F.V.

Spirits of the Cloth

Spirits of the Cloth
Contemporary African American Quilts

CAROLYN MAZLOOMI

PREFACE BY FAITH RINGGOLD
FOREWORD BY CUESTA BENBERRY

CLARKSON POTTER/PUBLISHERS
NEW YORK

PAGE 1: Detail from "The Color of Christmas"

PAGE 2: SIGNIFYIN'
BARBARA PIETILA
Baltimore, Maryland; 1994; 40 × 36 inches; cotton, appliqué, hand-quilted; photograph by Barbara Pietila

IN THE AFRICAN AMERICAN community we do not gossip, we "signify." This quilt shows how multilayered "signifyin'" can be. The two women on the back porch are the center of attention. The other figures—the young girl in the upper window, the man drinking coffee in the kitchen, the two women coming home from church, and myself looking out of the window in the foreground—are all curious about the conversation taking place on that back porch. I saw these two women on Sunday morning when I was driving through the neighborhood where I grew up. They reminded me of my mother and of the Sunday mornings when she talked over the back fence to our neighbor while the wonderful smells of baking bread, roasting meats, and spicy sweets floated on the morning air.

PAGE 3: Detail from "Watermelon Patchwork"

RIGHT: Detail from "Grandpa Blowing Booms for Susie and Spotty"

OPPOSITE: Detail from "The Chinaberry Tree"

PAGE 6: SOUTH AFRICA TRIUMPHANT
SANDY BARRETT HASSAN
Washington, D. C.; 1988–94; 40 × 40 inches; all cotton, pieced; photograph by Cecile Tolliver

"SOUTH AFRICA TRIUMPHANT" was conceived when Nelson Mandala visited Washington, D.C., upon his release from prison.

PAGE 7: Detail from "Memories of Childhood"

Copyright © 1998 by Carolyn Mazloomi

Published by Clarkson N. Potter/Publishers, 201 East 50th Street, New York, New York 10022. Member of the Crown Publishing Group.

Random House, Inc. New York, Toronto, London, Sydney, Auckland www.randomhouse.com

CLARKSON N. POTTER, POTTER, and colophon are trademarks of Clarkson N. Potter, Inc.

Printed in China

Design by Margaret Hinders

Library of Congress Cataloging-in-Publication Data
Mazloomi, Carolyn.
Spirits of the cloth : contemporary African-American quilts /
Carolyn Mazloomi. — 1st ed.
Includes bibliographical references and index.
1. Afro-American quilts—History—20th century—Themes, motives. I. Title.
NK9112.M37   1998
746.46'08996073—dc21   97-44101
                                      CIP

ISBN 0-609-60091-5

10   9   8   7   6   5   4   3   2   1

First Edition

Acknowledgments

THIS BOOK would not have been possible without all the talented and dedicated members of the Woman of Color Quilters Network. You are my extended family. This book is a testament to the value of our connectedness in our work and in our lives, and will remain as a legacy for future generations. To my dear friend and mentor Marie Wilson, your spirit will always surround me.

I am indebted to Cuesta Benberry and Beverly Guy-Sheftall, who always believed in the importance of this project, and never doubted for a moment that it could be done. Special thanks to Patrice Kelly for her help with editing, and for encouraging me to not give up on this book when I felt as though everything was falling apart. To Virginia R. Harris, Toni Smith, and Cathleen Bailey, thank you for lending your editorial and writing skills.

I am grateful to my editor, Annetta Hanna, for her patience, calm assurances, optimism, and guidance. Thank you to designer Maggie Hinders for making this book look so gorgeous. Thanks also to Joan Denman, Andrea Connolly Peabbles, and John Son at Clarkson Potter.

Finally, special thanks to my husband, Rezvan, for always allowing me the freedom to spread my wings and follow my dreams.

Contents

Preface

AS I WORKED ON THIS QUILT I began
to hear old songs of memories, prom-
ises, blues, and faith. I could hear the
struggle in each song, but also the hope.
Wouldn't it be great if we, as a people,
could come together and make a song
as this quilt did?

WHEN Carolyn Mazloomi, the noted quiltmaker and founder of the
Women of Color Quilter's Network, told me she was writing *Spirits of
the Cloth* to celebrate contemporary African American quilters, I was thrilled. But
when she asked me to add a few words to the opening pages and sent me the pictures of the beautiful quilts that are in this book, I felt overjoyed and profoundly
honored to be associated with such an important project.

Spirits of the Cloth showcases a breathtaking collection of African American
quilts. These pieces are as important to the history of African American art as
they are to the canon of American quiltmaking. They are not limited to any particular technique, medium, or school of thought. Rather, they reflect a diversity
of innovative techniques and media and a myriad of personally and culturally significant influences reflecting every aspect of our experience.

In viewing these works, it is important to keep in mind the struggle that Carolyn Mazloomi has had over the years with some who would narrowly define the
African American quilt. Let it be known that it is the quiltmakers, and not anyone else, who determine what the quilt art of their time and culture will be. Let
it also be known that African American quiltmaking is an American art and is as
rich and diverse as we are as a people. When Africans first arrived in America
with the Spanish and Portuguese explorers and slave traders in the early 1500s,
they came without wealth or material possessions. But they possessed the intellectual, spiritual, and cultural power to stamp an indelible imprint on American
life. Along with jazz, quilting is the uniquely American contribution to world art
that bears the legacy of our African heritage and carries it into our common
future. Created by some of the most remarkable artists alive today, this collection
of quilts is a testament to the virtuosity of African American art in one of its
greatest, and most heartfelt, forms.

—FAITH RINGGOLD

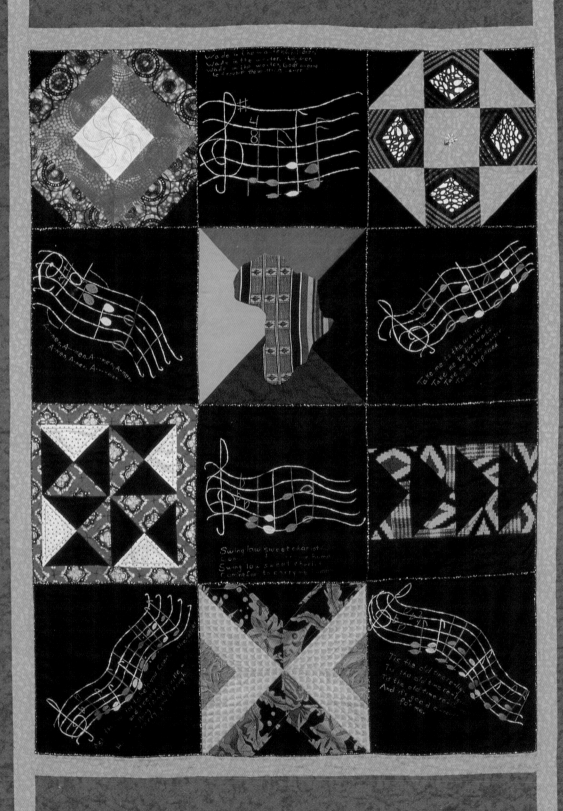

Foreword

CAROLYN MAZLOOMI'S importance in the African American quilting community is simply unrivaled. There is no one more closely identified with the promotion of contemporary African American quilts; as quilt artist, educator, and activist, her influence is pervasive and profound. Before her visionary gathering together of the Women of Color Quilter's Network in 1984, black quilters were isolated from one another and ignored by the wider public. They were separated from mainstream white quilters, and even within their own communities they often had little knowledge of each other's works.

This fragmentation actually intensified in the late 1970s when a number of white scholars discovered African American quilters and quilts. These academics selected a specific regional segment of black quiltmakers and conferred upon them the status of the true African American quilters. Only those quilts that conformed to certain criteria were considered to be authentic. The use of bright colors, large quilt patches, big stitches, and asymmetrical piecing unmistakably identified a quilt as being of African American origin, according to the scholars, who asserted that elderly southern black women, the genuine African American quilters, were the last of a dying breed, as young black women were not making real quilts.

In response, Mazloomi set out to document the broad range of works produced by African American quilters. She knew that the respected scholars were not motivated by any desire to denigrate African American quilters. Instead they were guilty of an innocent arrogance. They believed that through their scholarly analysis they could determine certain qualities that were inherent in the work of black, as opposed to white, American quilters. But ironically, because these scholars discounted the larger, more diverse body of African American quilters in favor of a small subgroup, their impact on the community they sought to recognize was adverse. Black quilters whose works did not conform to the scholars'

ABOVE: *Detail from "O'Kelley's Bonding"*
OPPOSITE: *Detail from "Summer's Splendor"*

10

criteria were relegated to an artistic limbo, where their quilts were regarded as neither authentic African American nor mainstream American fabrications.

Carolyn Mazloomi's credentials, both academic and experiential, made her the ideal person to challenge these skewed theories. She was determined to dissolve the artificial barriers that were being used to separate, even segregate, African American quilters within their own domain. Whether the quilters made utilitarian strip quilts or the most avant-garde art studio quilts, naive folk art quilts or traditional block bed quilts, whether the quiltmakers were old or young, whether they had southern rural roots or were reared in urban settings, Mazloomi reiterated the encouraging word that they were all authentic expressions of African American art and craft.

As black quilters embraced Mazloomi's inclusive approach, they were able to reclaim what was rightfully theirs. As their work received validation and respect, they were infused with a new spirit of confidence. Urged to acknowledge their own creativity, African American quiltmakers began to produce an amazing array of imaginative designs. Into their quilts they incorporated bold political themes, nostalgic childhood memories, and candid reflections of what it means to be black in America. They honored historical black American heroes and heroines, revisited their African heritage, and in countless other inventive ways expressed their originality. Carolyn Mazloomi's role in inspiring this freedom of expression cannot be overstated.

On the pages of *Spirits of the Cloth* are recorded some of the most visually exciting, the most originally conceived, the most captivating quilts being made today. Readers will see stark abstractions, storytelling pictorials, "slice of life" compositions, and uninhibited explorations of color, texture, and form. These works will dazzle the eye, as this book reveals the spirit of creativity that exists in the contemporary African American quilt world, a veritable "spirit of the cloth."

—CUESTA BENBERRY

Introduction

THROUGHOUT AMERICA there are families that have held on to quilts for generations and cherished them not for their function, but for the memories they embody. I vividly remember sleeping under quilts that weighed so much, I could hardly move beneath them. Warm and snug, I could look at the patches and associate each one with a family member, living or deceased. There was a patch from Aunt Flo's church dress, and looking at it brought back the sight of her all dressed up in her Sunday best. There were pieces of my mother's crisp green satin party dress and my uncle's red plaid hunting shirt, soft from wear. The patches of the quilt were our genealogy, the link between the generations of our family. They were the tangible reminders of our family's stories, rituals, and celebrations.

Tying the past to the present, quilting extends far beyond any one family, however. The African American quilting tradition is in fact centuries old, dating back to America's colonial period. The assumption that enslaved Africans arrived on these shores with nothing of their own refers only to their lack of material possessions. African slaves brought with them wisdom, abilities, and certain skills, including the techniques of appliqué, piecing, and embroidery. The peoples of western Africa had been wearing fine silks and cottons woven and sewn in elaborate patterns long before any European contact. The techniques of appliqué, piecing, and embroidery had been used for centuries. While there is no documentation of the three-layered bed quilt that we now construct, Africans were familiar with the techniques required to make piecework. The Hausa people of Nigeria, Chad, and Sudan made pieced and quilted armor for riders and horses for protection during battle, and the appliquéed banners of old Dahomey (modern Benin) are acknowledged as history preserved in fabric. The descendants of those taken from Africa and born into slavery used their needle skills to create decorative and utilitarian pieces for their masters as well as themselves. There are exquisite examples of antique quilts in museums across the nation whose origins have been attributed to Southern women of European extraction, but if those quilts had voices, they might well speak of dark hands that manipulated tiny pieces of fabric with nearly invisible stitches.

Descendants of these unknown artists, the quilters featured in *Spirits of the Cloth* are generally members of the Women of Color Quilter's Network, the oldest nationally organized African American quilt group in the United States. The Women of Color Quilter's Network (WCQN) came into being in 1986 as I made a commitment to preserve quiltmaking in the African American community. My employment required that I travel throughout the country, and I always sought out quilt exhibitions. After attending countless exhibitions, I began to feel isolated: I never found work that I could identify as my own experience, and I never saw other African Americans in attendance. Samplers began to lose their appeal, repetitive floral patterns no longer were enough to please my soul.

I placed an ad in a nationally circulated quilt magazine asking African American quilters to write to me. Nine women warmly answered that ad. As we communicated, I realized that in addition to sharing the same heritage, we all shared the same sense of isolation from the mainstream quilt community. Each women also believed quilting to be a dying art form within the African American community. Some were members of quilt guilds, but each was the only African American in her guild. What they created was not always well received by their fellow guild members, who could not understand what these quilts were all about. African American quilters clearly needed acceptance and affirmation to sustain their creativity. They found it in "the Network," which became a home where

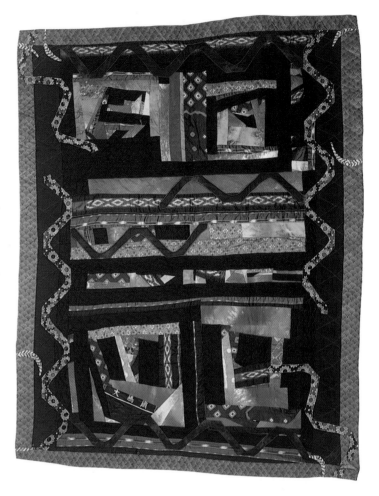

NATURE'S SONG
EDJOHNETTA MILLER
Hartford, Connecticut; 1996; 52 × 69 inches; cotton, silk; photograph by John Ryan

INSPIRED BY the warmth and color of Bahia Brazil, I used hand-painted silk throughout my quilt. I wanted to capture the colors of the morning sunlight, and the energy and beauty of the city and its people.

OPPOSITE: *Detail from "Aunt Alzeda's Sunday Concerts"*

CARAVAN
CAROLE HARRIS
*Detroit, Michigan; 1994; 50 × 50 inches; cotton,
machine quilted; photograph by Bill Saunders*

I USUALLY START OUT with something in mind, a sketch or an idea. As I play or work in a very intuitive, spontaneous way, other ideas and motifs emerge that want to be interpreted or want to be included.

OPPOSITE: *Detail from "Gullah Series"*

there was freedom to work in all styles and techniques, whatever the skill level. Like wildfire, news of the Women of Color Quilter's Network spread and over the next ten years membership grew to more than 1,500 quilters and enthusiasts.

The personal sense of isolation so many of us experienced was in part the result of a larger debate about African American quilts. In the late 1970s scholars attempting to codify the art form identified certain aesthetic characteristics based on a small group of quilts that were distinct from traditional European patchwork quilts. These experts defined African American quilts by such traits as vertical stripes, bright colors, asymmetry, improvisation, symbolic forms, multiple patterns, large stitches, and large design elements. Parallels to West African textiles were cited and it was asserted that these were evidence of an unconscious cultural memory of Africa. While many scholars embraced this criteria for defining African American quilts, others found it narrowly stereotypical. WCQN members scoffed at the phenomenon of outsiders creating the definition for something alien to their own cultural references. Nevertheless, that definition was accepted by collectors. Quilts that fit the narrow criteria were studied, preserved, collected, and celebrated as the definitive style for African American work, leaving all other styles unnoticed and unappreciated. Ironically, two studies conducted within the Women of Color Quilter's Network documented that less than 2 percent of members quilted in the "approved" improvisational style.

It was the groundbreaking research of quilt scholar Cuesta Benberry that debunked the myths surrounding African American quilts. Engaged in the study of quilt history for more than thirty years, Benberry's investigations have been conducted primarily in African American quilt history. Her 1992 exhibition and accompanying catalogue, "Always There: The African American Presence in American Quiltmaking," included quilts ranging from the slave-made to contemporary, and supported her claim that African American quilts are as diverse as the people themselves. This exhibit proved that there is a wide spectrum of quilts in the African American community, encompassing a variety of techniques and styles.

The personal experiences of African-American quilters have now been validated by scholarly recognition. But there is still much to be done. Unscrupulous collectors continue to perpetuate outdated stereotypes of African American quilts. And I still hear of rural quilters selling their work for as little as $20 or $30 to collectors and scholars who know that their true market value is in the thousands of dollars. In response, the Women of Color Quilter's Network has established a special outreach program to educate African American quilters around the country about the cultural significance as well as the monetary value of what they create. Initially, we worked with senior citizens, but our workshops are now designed to be 4, with elders teaching young people to appreciate their cultural heritage.

A growing appreciation for the African American sense of design, coupled with a scarcity of work, has made contemporary African American quilts among the most sought after of all collectibles. This book showcases a dazzling range of quilts and profiles the quiltmakers, providing a forum for their stories, their memories, and their experiences of sorrow and celebration. These quilts, like any art, serve as primary transmitters of the cultural, political, social, and spiritual values by which their artists live. The quiltmakers in *Spirits of the Cloth* are "fiber griots," whose voices are unique in the world of American quiltmaking. Their works are prose, poetry, and songs captured in cloth, eliciting an emotional response from the viewer. The artistry demonstrated here is proof of the vast wealth of talent and ingenuity preserved and inherited by a distinctive people whose roots stretch from the coasts of America to the shores of Africa.

Visions of Africa

D ESPITE the forced migration of our ancestors from Africa to the Americas, with all the ravages of the Middle Passage and its aftermath, African Americans over the centuries have maintained a deep spiritual connection to our homeland. The exodus of Africans produced slave populations in the United States, the Caribbean, and Latin America, a process of dispersal that would later be called the "African

ABOVE: Detail from "Egyptology"

OPPOSITE: RHYTHM IN MY SOUL, THE DANCER
SHERRY WHETSTONE-MCCALL
Kansas City, Missouri; 1992; 30 × 40 inches; cotton, beads, feathers; photograph by Neal Ray

MY FIRST EXPLORATION IN creating relief-form textile art, this piece incorporates movement, rhythm, and vibrant colors. To date this is my only image in which the main subject is painted instead of being made from fabric. The stipple quilting in the yellow area took sixty hours to complete. The leaves have wire inside them, allowing them to be shaped and twisted to create the illusion of movement. "Rhythm in My Soul, The Dancer" is currently on a three-year loan at the U.S. Embassy in Malawi, Africa.

Diaspora." The Diaspora is the single shared experience of these African peoples; it is the connective thread that ties us all together. Whether acknowledged or not, we have a common history, a history so painful that our collective unconscious still seeks healing from that experience—hence our interest in Africa. And as our vision of the Motherland increasingly becomes a force for healing, it is appropriate that quilt artists turn to this theme as a subject. ✳ The artists presented in this chapter are among those who are consciously seeking a reconnection with Africa. It is fitting that they use the art of quiltmaking, an art descended from African artisans, as "the tie that binds." They use their quilts as a medium to tell of the important links between our lives today and those of our ancestors. Although some white and black scholars, and many general observers, have assumed that African cultural traditions did not survive the profound disruptions of slavery, there are innumerable elements of African American culture that can be traced back to Africa. These have expressed themselves in our music, in our language, in our child-rearing practices and forms of worship, and even in our hairstyles, and so it would seem obvious that our material arts, such as quilting, would also contain them. ✳ Many of the artists here have also made pilgrimages to Africa and to other parts of the world where African peoples were dispersed during the slave trade. In their statements they speak eloquently about the powerful effect these trips made on their lives and on their art: they now use ornaments and fabrics like cowry shells, kente cloth, and mud cloth; they fashion masks; and they use the history of Africa to establish a tie with their ancestral past. ✳ Perhaps the most profound echoes of African culture in the Diaspora are found in the area of religion and spirituality, as Carole Y. Lyles's quilt "Dreams of Africa: African Portrait #1" explicitly affirms. The African belief in a supreme being with male and female intermediaries was maintained in the New World among blacks in the United States, the Caribbean, and South America, even as they embraced Christianity. Their ability to sustain an African religious iconography was especially strong wherever Catholicism was practiced because of the religions' similar uses of intermediaries. African deities were, for example, identified with Catholic saints in Brazil and Cuba in the practice of Santeria and Candomblé. Betty Leacraft's "Exu-Guardian of the Crossroads" was inspired by a trip to Bahia, Brazil, and by her knowledge of the Candomblé religion, which Afro-Brazilians still practice, while Michael Cummings's quilt "Haitian Mermaid" pays homage to the Yoruba goddess Yemaja, the goddess of the sea. The mermaid has "locks," a hairstyle that dates back to ancient Egypt, and she is positioned in front of a figure reminiscent of the Egyptian god Horus. Yet the piece also contains borders and decorative elements very much like the ones that might be found on an old American quilt. ✻ The works in this chapter often combine African symbols, themes, and fabrics with traditional American design elements. African uses of pattern, color contrast, and balance imposed on a Western art form is, in fact, a common element in African American culture. This juxtaposition of elements, ideas, and ornamentation from our ancestral homeland, with others borrowed from our recent history in the United States, characterizes the vision of the Diaspora of many artists. Adriene Cruz's "Tutu Egun—For the Ancestors," for example, recalls a libation prayer that the Yoruba people chant before any community or family event to honor their ancestors. Yet the bold use of color and the ragged symmetry of this piece also recall the inventors of ragtime, who took a traditional form of music and infused it with an African element—"ragged time," or irregular measures, to create a new art form. ✻ Other quilts similarly celebrate African influences

ABOVE: *Detail from "Kuba Circles on the Water"* OPPOSITE: *Detail from "Khemetic Paradise"*

upon our music. Betty Leacraft crosses the line between traditional and contemporary quilting with "Berimbau." The quilt is the textile embodiment of the stringed instrument used to accompany *capoeira*, the Afro-Brazilian martial arts form. Betty was moved to create this quilt after a trip to Bahia, the section of Brazil with the greatest retention and presence of the African culture. ✳

The recent interest in using African fabrics such as kente and mud cloth brings African American quilters just a bit closer to the Motherland. Carole Y. Lyles's "Dreams of Africa: African Portrait #1" and "Cowry Shells #1" by Janet Waters Bailey are examples of the vibrancy, color, and texture that African cloth makes possible. ✳ The reclamation of African-centered cultural practices, such as body ornamentation and the making of masks, is also manifest in African American quilts. Dindga McCannon's "Mask #45," Sandra Smith's "The Hood," and Marie Wilson's "Shield of Our Fathers" make exquisite use of mask imagery to recall Africa. Cynthia H. Catlin's "Big Hair" celebrates the artistry of African hair sculpture, an art form still very much practiced and admired by African Americans today. African history is evoked in Zene Peer's "Benin King," which celebrates the royalty of ancient Africa. There are also the reminders that Egypt was an African civilization in Myrah Brown-Green's "Khemetic Paradise" and Gerry Benton's "Egyptology," where the use of Egyptian symbols, hieroglyphs, and portraiture coupled with African fabrics makes a strong statement. Ida Schenck's "Trance Dance" recalls the San people of

ABOVE: *Detail from "Cowry Shells #1"*
RIGHT: *Detail from "Haitian Mermaid"*
OPPOSITE: *Detail from "Spirit in the Night"*

South Africa before the arrival of the Europeans; her fluid dancers on a calming violet background are themselves entrancing, and the spiritual as well as the social nature of dance in African culture is clearly acknowledged. Tina Brewer's "Glow From the Motherland" has as its principal image the Sankofa bird, which has special symbolic significance for African people; the quilt underscores the importance of African Americans knowing their own history. ✳ Our links to an African past are especially poignant when traveling to Africa, as many of the quiltmakers gathered here recall. Viola Burley-Leake's "Village Figure" and Edjohnetta Miller's "Spirit in the Night" were both inspired by returns to the Motherland, which they experienced as deeply spiritual and transformative. ✳ That African Americans maintain a spiritual connection to "home" is evident in much of our creative expression. The connective thread of a common ancestry and a brutally painful shared historic experience forges a powerful bond among us. African American artists explore this commonality as a means of expression and as a source of healing. The healing becomes communal, a very African cultural characteristic, when they share their exploration and revelation through their work. The naming of ourselves as an African people (as well as American) and the search for a connection to our past ground us in our history, keep alive the memory of our rich cultural heritage, and affirm our identity, which is critical to our spiritual, psychic, and emotional health.

◀ EGYPTOLOGY
GERRY BENTON

Pittsburgh, Pennsylvania; 1995; 42.5 × 42.5 inches; cotton; photograph by Iris Parker

EVERY YEAR THE AFRICAN American Heritage Quilter's Guild sponsors a challenge quilt. This quilt was my submission for 1995. I chose to use Egyptian culture as the theme for my wall hanging. Egypt is often mentioned separately from Africa, when it is in fact part of the same continent. My fabric selections included pieces of Egyptian scenes, which I placed at the centers of the stars. I designed and embroidered Egyptian symbols and added them to the quilt. Historically, the use of stars has been important to both Africans and African Americans as a source of guidance and direction.

MASK #45 ➤
DINDGA McCANNON

New York, New York; 1994; 50 × 25 inches; leather, mud cloth, shells, snake skin, cotton, found objects, lace; photograph by Dindga McCannon

WHEN I PAINTED ON canvas, the mask was one of two nonhuman forms I used as a subject. I don't remember why or when I decided to use masks in quiltmaking, but I know it was a happy day because I could then translate a flat form into three dimensions. This mask took on a life all its own and grew to be much more than I intended. I felt free to use all kinds of materials with absolutely no restrictions; this was music to my artistic soul. When I use masks in my work, I feel as though I'm borrowing from my ancestors to make art for the present.

SPIRIT IN THE NIGHT
EDJOHNETTA MILLER

Hartford, Connecticut; 1995; 55 × 54 inches; cotton;
photograph by John Ryan

"SPIRIT IN THE NIGHT" was inspired by
my last trip to Ghana. After working with
textile artists for eight hours a day, it was
refreshing to sit on the porch in the
evening and reflect on the day's events. I
would look up into the deep indigo sky
and feel a warm and wonderful spirit surrounding me, saying, "Welcome home."

24

◄ BENIN KING
ZENE PEER

Milwaukee, Wisconsin; 1992; 16 × 5.5 inches; cotton; photograph by Bill Simmons

THE KINGS OF ANCIENT Africa were responsible for both spiritual security and civil order. This hand-embroidered piece was inspired by the beauty and majesty of one such sovereign. His subjects created great works of art that symbolized his power, wealth, and sacred status. The colors around his neck symbolize his high rank, and the crown of beads indicates that his head is holy (West Africans believe the head is the temple, the sacred shrine of the body).

RITES OF PASSAGE ➤
EDJOHNETTA MILLER

Hartford, Connecticut; 1996; 53 × 63.5 inches; cotton, Nigerian indigo, silk; photograph by John Ryan

WHILE WATCHING a rehearsal for the Sankofa-Kuumba African Dance Ensemble, I was enthralled by the colors of their costumes and the fluid movement of their bodies. I wanted to create a quilt for them to dance under, dance on, and embrace as they go through the "rites of passage" into adulthood.

KUUMBA MANDALA
FRANCELISE DAWKINS

Glens Falls, New York; 1993; 33 inches in diameter; silk, cotton, and velvet; photograph by David Dawkins

IN KISWAHILI, *kuumba* means creativity. *Mandala*, which means circle in the Sanskrit language, symbolizes centering and completion. My piece is a visual chant of the universe as I perceive it, echoed in the dance of ancestral spirits.

▲ SHIELD OF OUR FATHERS
MARIE WILSON

Brooklyn, New York; 1994; 44 × 54 inches; cotton;
photograph by Theobald Wilson

THE CENTRAL IMAGE HERE is an adaptation of a Mbula-Ngula, a figure made by
Bakota tribesmen in Gabon, Africa. The
originals are made of a wooden armature
covered with sheets of beaten copper or
brass, and their function is to protect
tribal ancestors from the effects of evil.
They are displayed atop the baskets or
boxes that contain the skulls of deceased
chieftains. The surrounding motifs are
Adinkra symbols from Ghana. These designs were originally used to decorate
funerary clothes; now they are used for
many other occasions. There are hun-
dreds of Adinkra symbols representing
ideas and emotions, like courage, unity,
defiance, law, and slavery, or proverbs,
such as "Turn back, you can undo your
mistakes." In addition to conveying a
message, these symbols enhance any
object they decorate.

▲ DREAMS OF AFRICA:
AFRICAN PORTRAIT #1
CAROLE Y. LYLES

Columbia, Maryland; 1996; 36 × 40 inches; cotton,
machine quilted; photograph by Isaac Jones

THIS IS THE FIRST in a series of collaborative works. I acquired the batik used in
this piece over fifteen years ago, because
I recognized the African man depicted as
a brother. When I saw it, my spirit felt as
if it were being called home. As I worked
on this quilt collage, I felt a growing
sense of spiritual completion. I was
bringing all of who I am as an African
American artist to this collaboration with
an African artist I might never meet, but
whom I know to be my spiritual partner.

◄ The Hood

Sandra Smith

Silver Springs, Maryland; 1994; 20 × 27 inches; cottons, collection of Kathy Kalifian; photograph by David Caras

"The Hood" was inspired by an improvisational quilt class that I took in 1994. This poster-size quilt was made from my favorite scraps. The goal in making this quilt was to play with colors and textures, and to create something in a single day. The quilt also represents two firsts for me: it was the first quilt I'd designed without a template, and it was my first Afrocentric quilt.

Black Quilt #8 ➤

Jim Smoote

Chicago, Illinois; 1989; 33 × 43 inches; acrylic on appliquéd, pieced, and quilted satin, Pellon, cotton backing; photograph by Jim Smoot

"Black Quilt #8" is a composition of fifteen figures. Each figure is rendered in a different spotted pattern, which is also reflected in the border. The stylized figures are based on female fetish figures found in West African sculpture.

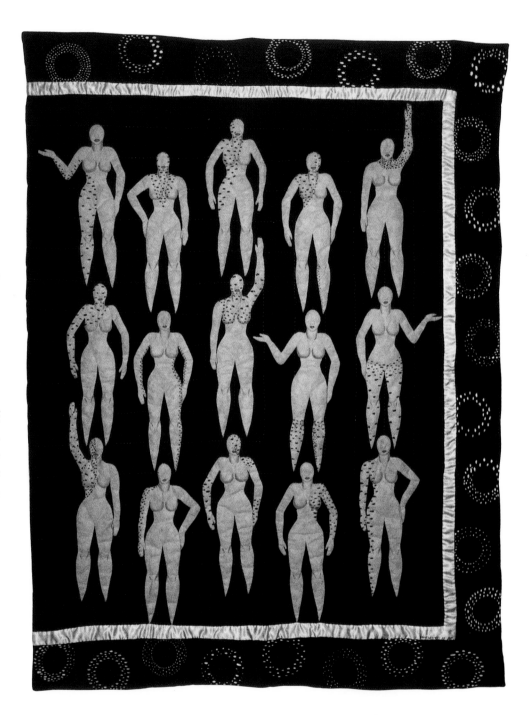

◄ Big Hair
Cynthia H. Catlin

Aurora, Colorado; 1995; 47 × 54.5 inches; cotton, batik; photograph by John Bonath

THE CENTER OF THIS quilt is a hand-painted African batik panel from Cameroon. It is machine pieced and quilted with Adinkra symbols that represent valor, bravery, and a readiness to serve. I used it to celebrate African hair sculpture as an art that requires manual dexterity, patience, and artistry, as many of the styles are elaborate and time-consuming.

Cowry Shells #1 ►
Janet Waters Bailey

Baltimore, Maryland; 1994; 22 × 35 inches; cotton, shells; collection of Roland Clinton; photograph by Janet Waters Bailey

THIS QUILT WAS COMMISSIONED as a gift for a New York fashion designer. The cowry shells' design is reminiscent of bead appliqué for clothing. Cloth is a highly marketable commodity in Africa and is extensively traded, reaching far beyond the continent's shores. In ancient Africa, cowry shells were used as monetary exchange. Appropriately, the combination of African fabric and shells is a celebration of the richness of African culture.

▲ Haitian Mermaid
Michael Cummings

New York, New York; 1995; 84 × 84 inches; cotton, silk, beads, buttons, appliqué; photograph by Sarah Wells

This quilt pays homage to a Yoruba goddess who came to the New World with the African captives aboard slave ships—Yemaja, a deity of love, faith, and purity. Yemaja can also transform herself into a human. Because she is the goddess of the sea, with powers over land and water, the quilt presents her holding a large fish.

▲ Potholders and Dervishes Plus
Sandy Benjamin-Hannibal

Brooklyn, New York; 1996; 96 × 108 inches; cotton; photograph by Robert Wrazen

This is a reversible quilt made of a collection of fabrics from around the world, spanning a period of approximately thirty years. The back is a patchworked union of three batiked fabrics. Its center is a batiked panel from Senegal, West Africa, with an illustration of life in an African village. "Potholders and Dervishes Plus" gave me a great sense of freedom and joy. There were so many associations in this quilt for me: the subjects; the kinship of techniques; where the fabrics came from and how they got to me; the people who had worn or used larger parts of these smaller fabric strips; and the most satisfying of all—my mother, who had chosen the pieces and arrangement of fabrics used in three of the squares.

⋀ Trance Dance
Ida Schenck

Denver, Colorado; 1996; 60 × 64 inches; cottons;
photograph by John Bonath

"Trance Dance" was inspired by a trip to Cape Town, South Africa, where I became captivated by the rock paintings of the San people (called Bushmen by Europeans). I had seen a few examples of this art before—animal figures and hunters—but I had no idea how far back the history of this art and the people who created it went. Until about 2000 years ago, the San were Southern Africa's only inhabitants. Trance experiences are still a central ritual for the San, who believe that the trance activates supernatural strength. The oldest rock paintings come from southern Namibia and have been dated to 26,000 B.C.E. Similar paintings are also found on ostrich eggshells, the oldest of which have been dated as far back as 13,000 B.C.E.

◄ GLOW FROM THE MOTHERLAND
TINA BREWER

Pittsburgh, Pennsylvania; 1995; 44 × 47 inches;
cotton, lamé, netting; collection of Ann Kenderson;
photograph by Fred Kenderson

THE SANKOFA BIRD HOLDS great meaning in the history and survival of African
people, and it appears in many of my
quilts. The two death effigies are the
spirits of the ancestors, who are seen
through the black figure in the quilt's
center. Meant to reflect the African
American heritage, this quilt's warmth
represents how we feel when we truly
know our history—because when you
know where you come from, you won't
be what others call you.

KHEMETIC PARADISE ►
MYRAH BROWN-GREEN

Brooklyn, New York; 1995; 21 × 18 inches; cotton;
photograph by Richard Green

"KHEMETIC PARADISE" BEGAN AS a
learning piece about machine embroidery. Soon after I began working on the
small quilt, I found a natural affinity for
machine embroidery and continued experimenting with the technique. The
title is derived from the ancient name of
the kingdom of Egypt, Khemit. The
scarab shape in the center not only symbolizes the goddess Het Heru but is also
a sign for good luck. We, as human
beings, are sometimes very self-centered
in how we view the world. We tend to
take so many of God's other creatures for
granted. Everything is on this Earth for a
purpose. At the bottom of the quilt there
are creatures that represent the animal

kingdom. They also serve a purpose.
They have their own communities just as
we do. Sometimes we don't notice them,
or we take them for granted. I want to
remember that we are intrinsically linked
to the animal kingdom.

◀ TUTU EGUN—FOR THE ANCESTORS
ADRIENE CRUZ

Portland, Oregon; 1996; 60 × 38 inches; cotton, beads, shells; photograph by Keith Aden

BEING AN ARTIST IS a very special gift. This quilt was designed to show gratitude for the blessings and comfort that being an artist and quilting have given me. The title "Tutu Egun" is taken from a Yoruban libation prayer acknowledging one's ancestors before an event. I hoped that by creating this quilt in honor of my ancestors, they would continue to bless me with benefits from my work.

▲ Exu-Guardian of the Crossroads
Betty Leacraft

Philadelphia, Pennsylvania; 1989; 30 × 30 inches; cotton, satin, shells; photograph by Will Brown

THIS QUILT IS THE first piece I made when I returned from Bahia, Brazil. The Yoruba deity Elegba is known as Exu in the Candomblé religion, the belief system brought to Brazil by Africans of that ethnic group. Natural and stylized cowry shells along with the use of Elegba's colors, black and red, in multiples of his number, three, resonate throughout this piece. While constructing this work, thread endings were done in multiples of three as were any knots or other closures, which produced an unexpected sense of ritual as I completed the quilt. I also created this work in loving memory of my maternal grandmother, Sadie Artist Wills, who put the first needle and thread in my hands when I was five.

▲ Village Figure
Viola Burley-Leake

Washington, D.C.; 1985; 5 × 6 feet; cotton, silk, lamé; photograph by Viola Burley-Leake

IN WORKING WITH THIS quilt I recalled traveling in Africa and my feelings there of wonder and magic. I wanted to evoke a feeling of dignity, as well as present an interesting figure study with color and structure to entice the viewer. The black woman holding a bird in a fanciful, poetic composition displays qualities of beauty, inner strength, and magic.

Africa. These are usually embroidered by women, who use the designs to teach their children mathematics as well as mythological stories of creation. The series of overlapping circles symbolizes various spheres of social life: the individual, the family, the community, sources of women's power, the eternal dialogue with the forces of nature, and the feminine principles of universal order. The cowry shells are vestiges of fertility, prosperity, and ancestral wealth. Taken as a whole, this quilt is a direct tribute to the female mystical power.

BERIMBAU ➤

BETTY LEACRAFT

Philadelphia, Pennsylvania; 1991; 62 × 17 inches. Wall component materials: hand/machine sewn, cottons, metallic cording, cotton knit, batting, upholstery welting, cotton string, textile paint, natural and hand-painted cowry shells, Brazilian beads. Floor component materials: earth, natural palm fronds, natural and hand-painted cowry shells, Brazilian beads. Photograph by Will Brown

THIS QUILT, which has both wall and floor components, is a textile representation of the single-stringed bowlike instrument used to accompany *capoeira* Angola, the traditional martial art brought to Brazil by captured Africans from the ancient Kongo and Angolan kingdoms. The music of the berimbau was used to camouflage *capoeira* Angola, masking its deadly movements as a dance to keep its adherents from suffering reprisals from their Portuguese masters.

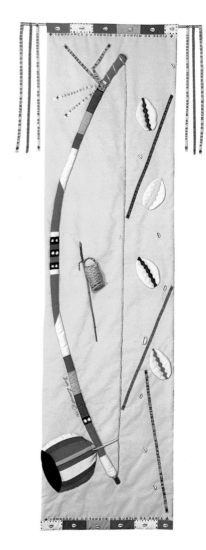

▲ KUBA CIRCLES ON THE WATER: SAVE ME FROM MY AMNESIA

L'MERCHIE FRAZIER

Roxbury, Massachusetts; 1992; 65 × 45 inches; cotton, metallic threads; photograph by L'Merchie Frazier

"KUBA CIRCLES ON THE WATER: Save Me From My Amnesia" is a quilt that echoes the energy retained from the experience of generations. The language of this "talking" cloth is taken from the textiles of the Kuba people in Central

Memories of Home

THE CONCEPT of home becomes profoundly important for displaced peoples. Despite assertions to the contrary, slavery did not erase African Americans' reverence for family and kin; there is much documented evidence of the great lengths to which slaves and former slaves would go to keep their families intact. Many of those who lived together on the plantations claimed each other as family in the

ABOVE: Detail from "Memories of Childhood II: Christmas"

OPPOSITE: GRANDPA BLOWING BOOMS FOR SUSIE AND SPOTTY
E. LORETTA BALLARD
East Point, Georgia; 1995; 36 × 48 inches; cotton, batik, machine appliqué, found fabrics; photograph by E. Loretta Ballard

MY MOST VIVID CHILDHOOD memories are of times spent with my grandparents. My grandpa, Jefferson Allen, a gentle, loving man, was my daily companion. In the late afternoon Grandpa, Spotty (our black and white fox terrier), and Susie (me) would sit under a big oak tree. I would watch him light up his pipe, packed with the tobacco he grew in the backyard, and blow smoke rings. Grandpa called these smoke rings "booms." Tiny gray rings moved slowly from his lips, then grew gradually larger and larger, until they disappeared into the sky.

absence of their blood relatives. After the Civil War, countless numbers of newly freed slaves set out to find family members who had been sold off to other plantations during slavery. The strength of those early families was transmitted to each new generation, establishing a tradition in the black community of close-knit and extended families. ✳ In fact, the institution of the family, in all of its extended variations, has been critical to the survival of blacks in a country where racial oppression, violence, poverty, and discrimination have been persistent and devastating. Memories of home and family have sustained us during difficult times and encouraged us in happy ones. Without this strong bond, it is difficult to say whether the horrors of slavery and the ensuing years of racial bigotry and oppression could have been survived. ✳ In our quilters' depictions of black family life, happy childhoods and stable, extended families are frequent themes. Barbara Pietila draws most of her inspiration from such memories. "Picnic Day for Barbara," for example, recalls the stories told by her friend Barbara of fun-filled outings with her grandmother. Pietila also captures lazy Saturday mornings with her own granddaughter in the quilt "Saturday Morning Cartoons." Peggie L. Hartwell's "The Chinaberry Tree" is a nostalgic recollection of her childhood on a farm in South Carolina, as is Michaeline Reed's "Memories of Childhood: Let's Play Dress Up," which recalls her carefree childhood when she dressed up in her mother's clothes. These pieces show a gentle side of the black experience that many African Americans know of but that is often little appreciated by those outside our culture. ✳ Dindga McCannon's "The Family" tells a more complicated story about the intertwined relationships exposed during family gatherings.

Common events like weddings, family outings, church activities, and funerals all provide opportunities to observe these complex interactions. Deaths of family members also evoke inspirational quilts, such as Edna Petty's "Ties That Bind." ✳ Peggie Hartwell's "African Skies and Southern Soil" is a portrait of a loving family with the father figure at the center holding up his piece of the sky, disputing the idea that black families are solely matriarchal. E. Loretta Ballard's "Grandpa Blowing Booms for Susie and Spotty" provides a loving portrait of a father figure and challenges the conventional notion that nurturing is the exclusive domain of women. Indeed, in the black family there have been and still are many fathers who, like Ballard's Grandpa, cook dinner, read stories, blow playful smoke rings, and offer children a view of the world from their place on the hill. Relationships among women are also important as subject matter for quilt artists: Sherry Whetstone-McCall's "Summer's Splendor" depicts the joy of sisterhood while evoking the lush beauty of the season. ✳ Holidays are family centered and fondly remembered among quilt artists, as in Reed's "Memories of Childhood II: Christmas," Whetstone-McCall's "There's Snowmen in the Forest," and Sandra Smith's "Happy Halloween." Reed's Christmas scenes are as endearing as a Norman Rockwell painting and as accurate a presentation of black family life as any other. Smith's ghoulish Halloween quilt recalls the childhood pleasures of dressing up in scary costumes and begging for treats. ✳ Though not obvious on the surface, Sandy Benjamin-Hannibal's "Native Americans" is also about

LEFT AND ABOVE: *Details from "Memories of Childhood"* OPPOSITE: *Detail from "Picnic Day for Barbara"*

family, specifically her part-Cherokee father, and offers a reminder of our largely invisible Indian heritage. Similarly, Marlene O'Bryant-Seabrook's "Gullah Series" celebrates the work of artist Jonathan Green, who drew upon memories of his childhood within the distinctive Gullah culture of South Carolina's coastal region. ✳ Hugs and kisses, long trips home, delicious meals around the kitchen table, and visits from "city folk" bearing gifts are the fabric of family, as are births, marriages, and deaths. These create the ties that bind—and sometimes strangle; here there is joy and sadness, hope and despair. Quilts are vehicles for remembering, and in these "family connection" quilts, the memory works on two levels. First, the quilt's imagery itself tickles the memories of the viewers, transporting them to another time and space; second, the fact that the piece of art is a quilt—a specially made functional piece of cloth—means that by its very nature it resonates with warm, cozy associations. Memory quilts feel as comfortable as your favorite slippers or the threadbare sweater you can never discard. ✳ As we approach the turn of the century, when many families are experiencing profound disruptions, it is not surprising that artists would evoke better times as a testament to the historic strengths of African American families. In some ways these artists are simply setting the record straight, since the black family structure has been much maligned in scholarly works and in the media. Reading their statements about the creation of these pieces brings to mind the African proverb "It takes a village to raise a child." Inspired by their own rich personal experiences and celebrating the African American family's capacity for survival and renewal, the quilts in this section are a testament to our creativity, endurance, resilience, and triumph.

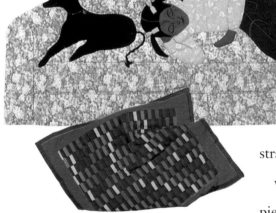

ABOVE: *Detail from "Saturday Morning Cartoons"*

THE CHINABERRY TREE ❯

PEGGIE L. HARTWELL

New York, New York; 1994; 40 × 53 inches; cottons; courtesy of Cheryl Sutton Associates; photograph by Konstantin

WHEN I WAS A little girl growing up on a farm in South Carolina, I loved the chinaberry tree that grew in the front yard of my grandmother's house. Actually, the chinaberry tree was like a family member. We children played in it, and the adults often sat in its shade and sipped lemonade as they planned the general running of the farm. At other times, the tree provided a social area for my grandfather and his male friends. They would sit and talk "men's talk," as my grandfather put it. The chinaberry tree represented the strength of our family and seemed to reinforce our family stability. So much happened around this tree. It stood royally, like an angel of mercy, often appearing to overflow with its own kind of love. And we loved it back. We were attracted to its outstretched limbs, so inviting and enticing. And sometimes those branches made us forget our chores, such as broom making. This quilt recalls one of those times, with my grandmother standing in the front yard, waving her thin arms in the air, scolding us, reminding us of our responsibilities. The trunk of the chinaberry tree would then be our refuge, a place to bury our shamed and teary faces.

◄ **MEMORIES OF CHILDHOOD:**
LET'S PLAY DRESS UP
MICHAELINE REED

Pittsburgh, Pennsylvania; 1994; 36 × 37 inches;
cottons; photograph by Iris Dawn Parker

I WANTED TO BRING back memories of those times in our lives when we didn't have a care in the world, when all the worrying was done by grown-ups and each day brought the promise of a new adventure. Little girls like to play dress up and I was no exception, so this quilt was the first in a series depicting the carefree life of a child.

◄ **MEMORIES OF CHILDHOOD**
JULIANNE MCADOO

Pittsburgh, Pennsylvania; 1991; 28 × 42.5 inches;
cottons; photograph by Julianne McAdoo

"MEMORIES OF CHILDHOOD" was created in response to an annual challenge by the African American Heritage Quilter's Guild. This particular year, we had to create a quilt using only six fabrics, four of which were preselected. I grew up in Pittsburgh and I have fond childhood memories of lazy summer days jumping rope double Dutch, and I called upon these memories to create a quilt as structured and as free as jumping rope.

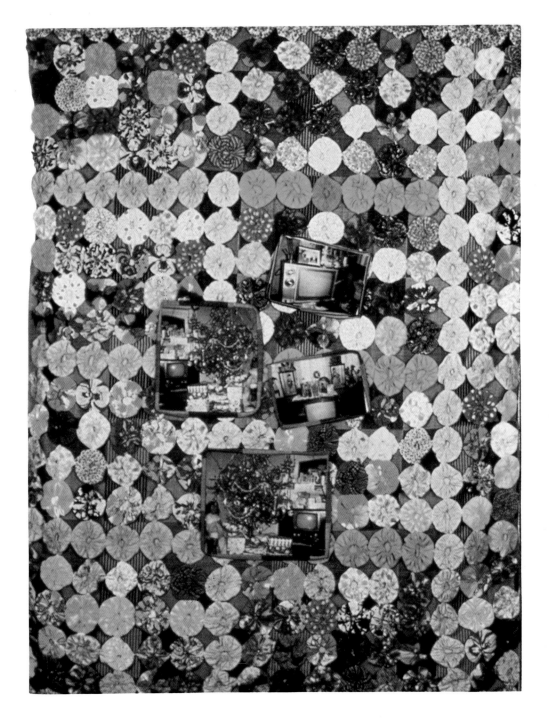

◀ DATE UNKNOWN
DEBORAH WILLIS

*Washington, D.C.; 1994; cotton, photo transfer;
courtesy of Steinbaum Krauss Gallery, New York City,
New York; photograph by Deborah Willis*

ONE CHRISTMAS IN THE late 1950s, I received my first camera. I had always wanted to use my father's camera to photograph family moments but hadn't been allowed to because it was "not a plaything" and was "too expensive." Many of my first photographs were taken in the house. From under the Christmas tree I photographed the television set, which was placed in front of the mantel. As I began to take photographs in the homes of my relatives, I became particularly interested in the placement of the television in the various rooms throughout their homes. I found the old negatives that I took years ago and printed them with contemporary photographs of television sets. In the quest to uncover and ask questions about television and the significance it had in my family, I found that my parents were the first to own a television and many members of my family would visit on weekends and evenings to sit and watch. One great-aunt made quilts as she watched. She gave me this yo-yo–inspired pattern. It is not a yo-yo quilt, but the pattern was popular among early quilters.

Gullah Series ➤

Marlene O'Bryant-Seabrook

Charleston, South Carolina; 1994; 81 × 98 inches; hand-transferred paintings, cotton, machine pieced, hand appliquéd, hand quilted; photograph by Marlene O'Bryant-Seabook

THIS QUILT DISPLAYS MIRROR images of the work of Jonathan Green. Green, who has pieces in numerous public and private collections, draws on recollections of his childhood to paint the vibrant pictures that reflect Gullah life. The Gullahs are the descendants of slaves brought to the sea islands off the coast of South Carolina and Georgia from Africa's "Rice Coast." Because they possessed the skills and knowledge to plant, cultivate, and harvest rice crops, large numbers of people from the same region were concentrated on the isolated, bridgeless islands. On the quilt, the silhouetted viewer's kente cloth hair bow and scarf and her cowry shell shoe clips are a reminder of the Gullahs' direct link to Africa.

▲ Memories of Childhood II: Christmas
Michaeline Reed

Pittsburgh, Pennsylvania; 1994; 36 × 38 inches; cotton, appliqué, hand and machine quilted; photograph by Dawn Parker

THIS QUILT IS ONE of a series celebrating the big moments in children's lives, particularly the anticipation and excitement of opening presents on Christmas Day. I wanted to make a quilt that captured the charm and flavor of the holiday season through the eyes of a child. This quilt gives expression to my own special memories of Christmas.

▲ There's Snowmen in the Forest
Sherry Whetstone-McCall

Kansas City, Missouri; 1996; cotton, pearls, feathers, twigs; photograph by Neal Ray Shoger

I ENJOY THE CHALLENGE of experimentation. In this piece, feathers and twigs were used as trees. Ceramic and mother-of-pearl buttons became snowmen. The two children have set off for a fun-filled day of snow sleighing. On the way, they discover several snowmen in the forest and decide it would be more fun to watch snowmen than to go sleighing. My son, Ronald, drew several snowman templates for me to use as quilting patterns.

ꕢ Picnic Day for Barbara
Barbara Pietila

Baltimore, Maryland; 1994; 65.5 × 47.5 inches; cottons; photograph by Barbara Pietila

ONE DAY, ON a fabric-shopping spree, my friend Barbara and I stopped to have lunch. My granddaughter was with us, and Barbara told her a story about taking bus trips with her grandmother as a little girl. They would travel on the bus, eat her grandmother's fried chicken and biscuits, and have their outing. My friend recalls always falling asleep in her grandmother's lap during the return trip home. I loved the story and made this quilt as a tribute to all happy childhood memories.

◀ Saturday Morning
Cartoons
Barbara Pietila

Baltimore, Maryland; 1993; 39 × 43 inches; cottons, hand appliquéd and quilted; photograph by Barbara Pietila

MY GRANDDAUGHTER LOVED TO come over on Saturday mornings and watch cartoons. She was always at odds with my poodle as to who would sit on the sofa: neither of them wanted to share. One morning, after they had been fighting for hours about who was going to sit on the sofa, I peeked in to find them both asleep at opposite ends. I took a picture of them sleeping together and made this quilt so that my granddaughter would be able to remember the day when she made peace with my dog.

◀ Ties That Bind
Edna J. Petty

East St. Louis, Illinois; 1994; 42 × 42 inches; cotton, silk, blends; collection of Rev. Joseph and Cheryl Anthony III; photograph by Edna J. Petty

THIS PIECE WAS INSPIRED by a loss. A colleague's mother passed away and Cheryl (the daughter) wanted an art piece that would represent her "mother, family, and God." The hand appliqués are of Cheryl, her husband, and their children. The ribbon begins and ends in the hands of an angel, who symbolizes the mother/grandmother and connects with the hands of Cheryl's family, thereby creating the "ties that bind." The beaded cross is symbolic of the entire family's involvement in the church. When Cheryl first saw the completed piece, she was overwhelmed.

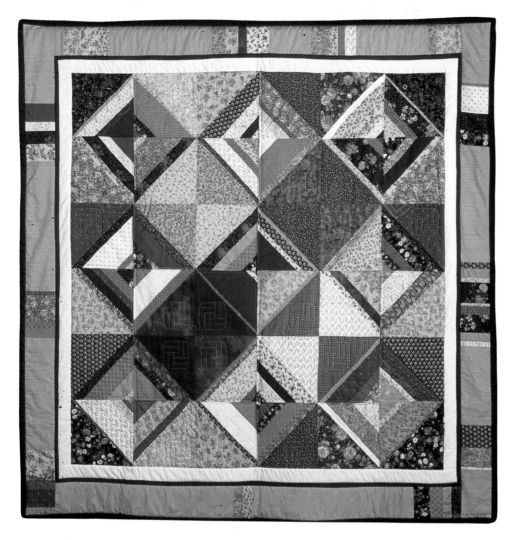

RHYTHMS OF LIFE: FROM THE CRADLE TO THE GRAVE ➤
EDNA J. PETTY

East St. Louis, Illinois; 1994; 64 × 52 inches; cotton, appliqué, machine quilted; photograph by Edna Petty

AS A FORMER PARENT educator, a mom, and an innate nurturer, I love children, people, life, and everything it has to offer. I especially love the way children think, react, and explore. They are naturally inquisitive. Many young parents fail to understand that and thereby force the child out of his natural rhythm. We all have a rhythm, and when we are out of sync with it, nothing seems to go right until we find the balance that keeps us together. I designed "Rhythms of Life" as a statement to young parents and children. A child can be born into this world under a cloud of doom or a cloud of glory. The image at the bottom is of a cradle/casket. Even though a child may not be physically dead, too often they are emotionally and creatively deprived if they are not nurtured, loved, and allowed to find their own life.

⌃ O'KELLY'S BONDING
VIVIAN M. WALKER

Hampton, Virginia; 1994; 56 × 56 inches; cotton; photograph by Stephen F. Gill

I HAVE ALWAYS ENJOYED a good relationship with my two children and their friends. So when our daughter invited my husband and me to visit her in her new apartment just outside of Baltimore, Maryland, we happily accepted. During our visit, some of her friends came over to watch a football game on television.

While we all talked and got to know one another, I worked on hand-stitching the band on my quilt, which I had brought with me. When I finished the stitching and enjoyed the moment of completion, I announced that I needed a name for the quilt. One of the young men present suggested that I call it "Bonding," because that was what we were doing that afternoon. Somehow that seemed to fit, and since his name is O'Kelly, I decided to name this quilt "O'Kelly's Bonding."

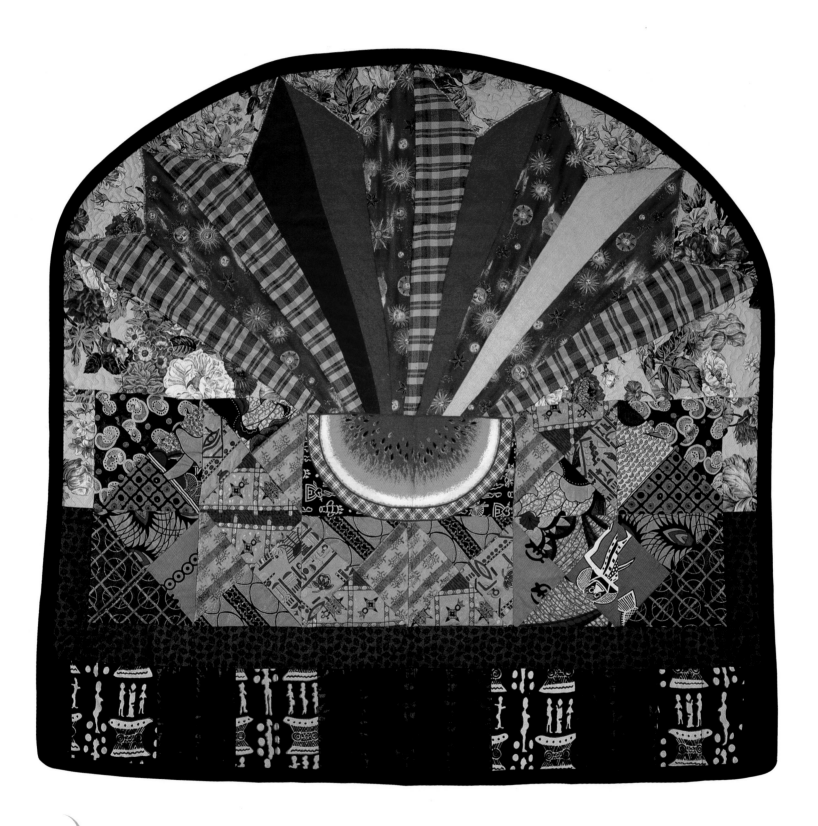

SPIRITS OF THE CLOTH

◄ WATERMELON PATCHWORK
ANA ARZU TITUS

*New York, New York; 1995; 50 × 60 inches; cotton;
photograph by Ernest Oliveri*

WATERMELONS UNITED MY family in a
Sunday morning ritual. I would travel
with my father and five siblings, by bus,
for three to five hours to buy watermelons in Indian villages. The Indians would
greet us as we exited the bus, each shov-
ing sliced samples of their watermelon at
us, claiming theirs was best. By the time
we made our selection, I looked as though
I'd swallowed an entire watermelon. I
would always fall asleep afterward, and
my father would hold me in his arms all
the way home. I love watermelon, but I
don't eat it. I have grown to dislike eating
and spitting at the same time. Yet it never
fails, anytime I attend a social function in
the summer involving black people, they
serve me watermelon.

SUMMER'S SPLENDOR ►
SHERRY WHETSTONE-MCCALL

*Kansas City, Missouri; 1994; 30 × 30 inches; cotton,
beads, buttons, found objects; collection of Francelise
Dawkins; photograph by Neal Ray Shoger*

THIS IS MY MOST colorful and whimsical quilt thus far. I enjoyed embellishing
the flowers with beads, silk ribbon
embroidery, and buttons; the little girl's
hair is created entirely from beads. I kept
thinking of myself and my oldest sister,
Patty, while working on this piece. We
were always finding fun things to do
together. What could be more fun than
playing in a field of flowers and trying to
find the biggest, prettiest one of all?

PEGGIE L. HARTWELL

*New York, New York; 1994; 95 × 55 inches; cottons;
photograph by Sara Wells*

WE WERE NURTURED, transformed, and made whole as a family. We were healed with our hope and kept safe through prayer. We were blessed with inspiration and the knowledge that, yes, there really was a love far greater than our own—just above our heads. This quilt is dedicated to all families.

THE FAMILY ▶
DINDGA MCCANNON

*New York, New York; 1992; 60 × 70 inches; beads,
buttons, cottons, blends, spandex; photograph by
Dindga McCannon*

THIS QUILT REMINDS ME of the typical wedding party. The two ladies in the back don't like each other. They haven't spoken in years, but have called a temporary "peace day" because their niece is getting married. The couple on the left have been together for thirty-five years and they hope their son, the groom, will finally settle down. The bride, who is not dressed yet, is one of those outgoing, "tell it like it really is" women. She probably shouldn't be getting married in the first place. Perhaps she is too independent, too visionary for her traditional Muslim husband. I also added children to the piece to represent the age spectrum of the generations.

HAPPY HALLOWEEN ❯
SANDRA SMITH

Silver Spring, Maryland; 1997; 35 × 44 inches; cotton, machine quilted; photograph by David Caras

HALLOWEEN IS MY FAVORITE holiday, so I made a quilt for the occasion. I've always loved buying pumpkins and looking for the goblins that come in October, so I've collected fabrics that contain these elements. Now I have so much Halloween-theme fabric that I've decided to make a series of quilts to celebrate this holiday.

▲ NATIVE AMERICANS
SANDY BENJAMIN-HANNIBAL

Brooklyn, New York; 1994; 50 × 50.5 inches; cotton, cotton blends, threads, sequins, seeds, tubular and terra-cotta beads; photograph by Robert Wrazen

"NATIVE AMERICANS" IS A tribute to my father, who was part Cherokee Indian. It is also a tribute to the many African Americans who share this same heritage. The batting extends beyond the quilt top to form the outer border. When the quilt top is viewed closely, one will see the batting peeping through. The back is cotton upholstery fabric. The whole-cloth part of the top is echo quilted. On the inner borders are quilted a buffalo, decorated horse, eagles, and symbols of rain clouds and friendship.

Healing: A Balm in Gilead

I N AN INSPIRATIONAL essay on the necessity of beauty in the lives of black women, "Aesthetic Inheritances: History Worked by Hand," feminist writer bell hooks describes the significance of quilt-making for her grandmother, Baba, for whom it was "a spiritual process where one learned to surrender. It was a form of meditation where the self was let go . . . it was an art of stillness and concentration, a work which

ABOVE: Detail from "The Blues"

OPPOSITE: HEALING SPIRIT
EDJOHNETTA MILLER
Hartford, Connecticut; 1996; 54 × 63 inches; cotton, machine quilted; photograph by John Ryan

THE WORLD NEEDS healing and peace. This quilt symbolizes the possibility of healing through warmth and realigning ourselves with Mother Earth. I chose these particular earth tones to visually convey a movement toward connecting with the powers of the universe.

renewed the spirit . . . a way to 'calm the heart' and 'ease the mind.'" In a variety of ways contemporary quilters also attest to the connection between the making of quilts and the attainment of inner peace. ✳ In "Come Into My Garden," which Frances Hare describes as a whimsical piece, there is a beautiful space, her "ideal thinking place," where she can read and heal and be shielded from the cares and snares of the world. Carolyn Cameron's "Winter Stream" attests to the healing power of her own art. Having suffered an injury as a young woman that prevented her from achieving her greatest ambition—becoming a classical ballerina—she now dances using fabric, which has movement, rhythm, sensuality, and mood. The colors and patterns of the fabric enable her to capture the "rippling stream of icy water, coursing its path through the earth, glinting and sparkling as it passes into sunlight, and darkening as it slips through winding crevasses." Adriene Cruz's "Meditation Quilt" was intended as a special yoga mat for meditation. During the course of creating it, she realized that she was grieving for lost loved ones. Making it enabled her to find peace, so that she now considers all her quilts to be meditation quilts. In her piece, vivid purples and blues, the colors of strength and faith, are infused with life-sustaining red, creating a visual representation of healing. ✳ Edjohnetta Miller's "Healing Spirit" suggests the possibility of healing through "our alignment with mother earth," which will bring balance and harmony to our lives. Sandra Smith's "Transitions" simply reminds us that life is about change; quilting allows her to absorb and use that

ABOVE: *Detail from "Come Into My Garden"*
ABOVE RIGHT: *Detail from "Transitions"*
OPPOSITE: *Detail from "The Blues"*

change gracefully. ✳ Not all of the healing that takes place here is within the artist; the viewer also can experience a positive energy flow, an opening up, a resolution, by viewing these works. Hare's abstract "garden" is warm and inviting, while Carolyn W. Cameron's "Winter Stream" is cool and releasing; the strong colors in Cruz's "Meditation Quilt" emit a power of their own. ✳ It is an important aspect of these pieces that quilting itself grew out of a very practical need to provide warmth. Quilts are unmistakably associated with healing, whether to cover the elderly to "keep their bones warm" or to cover a child to break a fever. We snuggle under them during bitter-cold winters, and we use them to provide comfort to any den or bedroom. It is perhaps fitting that quilters, working in a medium with deep roots in nurturance, are necessarily healed by their work. ✳ Here there is ample evidence of the therapeutic ways in which black women cope with stress and emotional upheaval. Quilts soothe our wounds, calm our spirits, and enable us to find solace in a world in which we are so often responsible for the needs of others. With our hands we have healed ourselves, blessed and nurtured others, and envisioned a new day.

⌃ WINTER STREAM
CAROLYN W. CAMERON

Kansas City, Kansas; 1996; 26 × 34 inches; cotton, paper; photograph by Carolyn W. Cameron

AS A YOUNG WOMAN, I trained as a dancer. My greatest wish was to become a classical ballerina. Unfortunately, I suffered an injury that prevented the realization of my dream. But I've learned to incorporate the movement, rhythm, sensuality, colors, and moods of dance into my quilt art. "Winter Stream" is such a piece, combining paper and fabric. The paper gives substance to the fabric, holding the rhythm, creating the flow; it molds the fabric. The colors and patterns of the fabrics form the rippling stream of icy water coursing its path through the earth, glinting and sparkling as it passes into sunlight, and darkening as it slips through winding crevasses.

THE BLUES ❯
CATHLEEN R. BAILEY

Pittsburgh, Pennsylvania; 1995; 15 × 18 inches; cotton, traditional mud cloth, coins, paper, buttons, ribbon, burlap, cotton balls, found objects, yarn; photograph by Cathleen R. Bailey

I NEEDED TO MAKE THIS little quilt after I saw a documentary on the blues, the singers, and the history of their difficult lives in work camps and on the railroads. The sadness of the documentary affected me deeply, but by creating this quilt I found the necessary outlet through which I could explore and release those strong feelings.

DIVINE GUARDIAN
ADRIENE CRUZ

*Portland, Oregon; 1996; 24 × 27 inches; cotton;
acrylic paint, beads, shells; photograph by Keith Aden*

I WANTED TO DO A piece on guardian angels, since mine seemed to be on a long-term vacation. At first, though, I was stuck finding the right approach for the design. Images of ancestors and children came to mind as a way to show the energy of angel work. Then I saw a photograph of Alonzo Davis's wonderful piece titled *Winged Spirits*, and something happened. After three attempts at painting the face of an angel, my angel finally came forth—a very special, kind, and fun-loving angel who showed me that if I accepted responsibility for my mistakes, I'd be able to move forward. Creating "Divine Guardian" was like going to confession. I confessed to all that was troubling me and found comfort working on the design and the many colors of her wing.

70

◄ TRANSITIONS
SANDRA SMITH

Silver Spring, Maryland; 1997; 72 × 78 inches; cotton, lamé, silk, machine quilted; photograph by David Caras

"TRANSITIONS" WAS INSPIRED by a course in isometric design. The quilt was originally named "Space Junk," but as the years passed by, many changes occurred in my life. My aunt Joyce died. I got a new job. I moved from Massachusetts to Maryland. I bought a house and went through a lot of personal changes along the way. Every time I looked at the quilt or picked it up to work on it, I reflected on all the things that had happened as time passed by, so I changed the name to "Transitions." It's amazing how much can happen in four years.

PRIMARILY BLACK AND WHITE ➤
DELLA COLLINS

Houston, Texas; 1993; 34 × 45 inches; cottons, seed beads, buttons, pearls; photograph by Della Collins

I MADE THIS QUILT during a very tense time in my life. Everything seemed to be going wrong all at once. I felt as if I were standing on a precipice, staring into a valley of darkness. Appropriately, this quilt was my first attempt at abstraction. Making it was like therapy; it helped me focus on something other than my problems. The quilt turned out well and my problems were eventually solved.

◀ MEDITATION QUILT
ADRIENE CRUZ

Portland, Oregon; 1993; 75 × 48 inches; cotton, shells, beads; collection of Joseph Cruz; photograph by Keith Arden

THIS QUILT WAS INSPIRED by yoga classes I'd taken with Konda Mason. I so loved practicing yoga with her that I decided to create a special yoga mat for meditation. My intention was to create a calm and soothing quilt, but as I began, I realized I was still hurting from the grief of lost loved ones—my stillborn son and a very dear cousin who had fallen to the ravages of AIDS. What started as a simple yoga mat became a pure meditation on the struggle between outward appearances and inner turmoil. I found peace creating this quilt, and now refer to all my quilts as meditation quilts.

COME INTO MY GARDEN ▶
FRANCES HARE

Rochester, New York; 1995; 59 × 61 inches; cottons; photograph by Frances Hare

THIS IS PURELY A whimsical piece, coming from a whimsical thought. I've often dreamed of having a garden or space where I could go and find peace and feel bliss. It would be my ideal thinking place. There would be birds carrying fanciful things, and the plants would have leaves that billow against soft winds. I would contemplate there. I would read there. I would heal there.

Sacred Space

For a people in bondage, the Judeo-Christian religion, with its emphasis on renewal and rebirth, became a source of tremendous comfort and release. Religion sustained us during slavery by helping us to cope with the oppressions in our daily lives. Forced to practice Christianity, enslaved Africans blended their beliefs from home with European religious practices. Numerous examples of the syncretism

ABOVE: Detail from "The Promise of Redemption Fulfilled"

OPPOSITE: THE TEACHER
ANA ARZU TITUS
New York, New York; 1996; 62 × 69 inches; cotton, machine quilted; photograph by Ana Arzu Titus
A SPIRITUAL LIFE is not the result of some natural instinct—it has to be taught and transferred from one generation to the next. I believe that one of our sacred duties is to take the time to teach the next generation. We need to pass on our spiritual wisdom about living as full human beings. How else will we transmit appreciation for life on this planet? This is what I'm trying to express in "The Teacher."

of African and European religious patterns appear throughout the Diaspora. The uniquely African American ring shout, the practice of vodun in Haiti, of Santeria throughout the Caribbean, and of Rastafarianism in Jamaica are examples of this syncretism. Francelise Dawkins's quilt "Jah's Peace" was, in fact, inspired by Jah, the God of the Rastas. The bright colors on the contrasting background affirm life; the prominent music symbol and the play on words in the title suggest that our unique music is almost celestial. ✴ The political history of African Americans has also been closely tied to religion. From Emancipation to the mid-20th century, churches were the only institutions that were our very own, places where African Americans could meet freely and exercise leadership. Sunday was our day for dressing up, for shaking off the dust of the fields and taking off the aprons that were our new badges of servitude. ✴ Over time our churches increasingly became political spaces, places where we could organize and protest. The civil rights movement of the 1960s was born in churches, as were many concepts that helped to define that volatile period. "Black is beautiful," the Black Madonna, and the daily admonishment to "keep the faith" were all nurtured in the black church. There, civil rights and labor leaders (many of whom were ministers) met with politicians, artists, and laypeople of all kinds to radically change America's public policy regarding black people. And though the struggles were many, we were sustained by a deep faith, one that allowed us to overcome in the same way our slave ancestors had. ✴ Chris Clark's "Sermon on the Mount" is among many of his quilts that have explicit biblical themes. The image of a black Christ delivering a sermon is testament to Clark's faith in God and to his perception of Christ as a black man. "The Promise of Redemption Fulfilled," which was designed by Peggie Hartwell and made by the children at St. Paul Apostle Church, celebrates Easter, the most significant holy day in Christendom. Biblical themes are also imaginatively illustrated in Yvonne Wells's "The Whole Armor of God," in which a passage from Ephesians is evoked to underscore the power of the Lord to protect us from harm. ✳ Though the religious experience of African Americans has been predominantly Christian, we have embraced other faith traditions. We have also sustained a sense of spirituality that is not necessarily tied to organized religion. Some-times our spirituality is akin to that of Native Americans, who revere the earth and its creatures, who sense divine power in all living things, and who are in touch with the balance and harmony of nature, as evoked in Helen A. Kearney-Thobhani's "Santa Fe Bargello." ✳ Patricia Johnson's "Fish Fantasy" recalls a similar belief system found in West Africa, which emphasized the profound

links between nature and humans. She also reminds us that organized religion is not the only route to spiritual expression. Tina Brewer's "All Life Begins in Darkness" seems to be a metaphor for both the creation story and the womb, while Michaeline Reed's "Flights of Fancy" is a testament to the power of the human spirit and its connections to other living things in the universe. As the quilts in this chapter reveal, religion and spirituality have been critically impor-tant to our survival as a people here and throughout the Diaspora. We have kept the faith.

ABOVE: *Detail from "The Promise of Redemp-tion Fulfilled"* OPPOSITE: *Details from "The Whole Armor of God"*

◄ PENTECOSTAL CROSS #5: IN THE GARDEN
CAROLE Y. LYLES

Columbia, Maryland; 1995; 44 × 56 inches; cotton; photograph by Isaac Jones

IN 1995, I BEGAN A series of spiritual works depicting the cross in a variety of settings. Each piece was designed to evoke the feeling of being in a sacred space or sanctuary. This piece was inspired by an old Baptist hymn in which the singer and Christ stroll through a garden early one morning. It is a song of joy, healing, and peace. In much Christian art, the cross is a scene of death and suffering. For me, it is also a symbol of love and redemption, which is the vision this work was designed to convey. The title of this series was inspired by the name of my church, the Pentecostal Baptist Church. The golden circle behind the cross symbolizes the divinity of Christ and the light that faith brings to our lives.

◄ MIDNIGHT STAR
DORIS PARKER

Los Angeles, California; 1996; 45.5 × 45.5 inches; all cotton; photograph by Doris Parker

"MIDNIGHT STAR" IS MY first original design, and I am very proud of it. I saw the material several years ago, cut out the diamond shapes, and then tucked them away, not knowing what I would do with them. It wasn't until I walked into a quilt shop at the end of 1996 and saw the background fabric that I knew I would use these pieces to create a star. On the way home I pictured an orange circle with a black center on a background of midnight sky, and all of a sudden it burst into a huge star full of spiritual meaning.

JAH'S PEACE ➤
FRANCELISE DAWKINS

Glens Falls, New York; 1992; 25 × 37 inches; silk, iridescent fabrics, cotton, velvet; photograph by Leonard's Universal Studio Photography

OBSESSIVELY REPEATING THAT I had to work on my "Jazz Piece" for a visual arts competition, I experienced a shift in consciousness when the mantra "Jah's Peace" revealed itself to me. Since "Jah" is the name of God for the Rastafarian people of Jamaica, I felt empowered to create a spiritual map interpreting the universality of jazz: Jah's Peace, Jazz Piece, Jah's Jazz!

◄ SERMON ON THE MOUNT
CHRIS CLARK

Birmingham, Alabama; 1994; 62 × 55 inches; cotton, acrylic paint; photograph by Chris Clarke

JESUS TRAVELED THE TOWNS around Galilee, speaking in each about the Kingdom of Heaven. One day He went up on a hillside and began to speak. A large crowd gathered and listened for hours. In the Sermon on the Mount, Jesus gave people a model to follow when they prayed. It was this model, the Lord's Prayer, that was revealed as part of His teachings. The words are as true today as they were for the people on that hillside in Galilee, and so this quilt celebrates the word of my Lord.

FISH FANTASY ❯
PATRICIA JOHNSON

Hampton, Virginia; 1996; 20 × 22 inches; cotton, appliqué; photograph by Na'Dere of Hampton

THIS QUILT WAS MADE during a workshop taken a few years ago. While working on this piece, I realized that some people confine spirituality to a book or church and fail to recognize the ever-present spirituality of their natural surroundings. When we open ourselves to nature's beauty, power, and intricacy, then spiritual lessons will come to us with little effort.

◄ SANTA FE BARGELLO
HELEN A. KEARNEY-THOBHANI

Littleton, Colorado; 1993; 76 × 80 inches; cottons;
photograph by Helen A. Kearney-Thobhani

THIS QUILT IS A celebration of the planet
Earth, so I used a strip-pieced bargello
technique to represent the various strata
of our planet. Beginning in the center of
the earth, we find white molten lava, represented by white fabric. Proceeding outward, we find an archaeological layer
depicted by a pottery fabric, then water,
sky, and fire. The stratum inhabited by
man is embellished with a family. The
layers continue through to the heavenly
bodies and the "black hole," represented
by black fabric. The purple fabric represents a past earth, regal and unpolluted.
And the vertical strips are cyclical, like
many of earth's processes.

FLIGHTS OF FANCY ➤
MICHAELINE REED

Pittsburgh, Pennsylvania; 1989; 25 × 34 inches;
appliqué, patchwork, ribbon, decorative machine
stitching; photograph by Iris Dawn Parker

A DEAR FRIEND BROUGHT a piece of
Japanese fabric back from California for
me. It was approximately 27 × 18 inches.
I challenged myself to use every inch of
the fabric and I succeeded. I had only a
2 × 3-inch piece left after the top was
completed! I enjoy adding extra touches
to my quilts, something different from
the ordinary. "Flights of Fancy" symbolizes the invincibility of the human spirit.
Our spirits live on in the face of trials and
tribulations to become even stronger.

◄ THE WHOLE ARMOR OF GOD
YVONNE WELLS

Tuscaloosa, Alabama; 1995; 70 × 96 inches; cotton; courtesy of Robert Cargo Folk Art Gallery; photograph by Robert Cargo Folk Art Gallery

I WAS INSPIRED TO make this quilt to illustrate what is needed to protect us from worldly enemies. It is drawn from the Book of Ephesians 6:13–17: "So that you may be able to stand your ground, you will need the sword of the spirit, helmet of salvation, shield of faith, breastplate of righteousness, buckle of truth and shoes of peace. With this armor, nothing can penetrate into it."

THE PROMISE OF REDEMPTION FULFILLED ➤
THE CHILDREN OF ST. PAUL APOSTLE CHURCH; DESIGNED BY PEGGIE L. HARTWELL

New York, New York; 1997; 10 × 13 feet; cotton, appliqué, machine quilted; photograph by Peggie L. Hartwell

THIS QUILT WAS MADE by the children of St. Paul Apostle Church in celebration of Easter. The blocks represent the Transformation (Christ talking with Moses and Elijah); Palm Sunday (Christ enters Jerusalem); Christ carrying the cross; Christ and Thomas, the Apostle; the Ascension; and the Pentecost. For Christians around the world, Easter is a celebration of the sanctity of the human soul. The resurrection was not only a visible sign of the redemption but also a confirmation of eternal life. Through the resurrection, we too will overcome death and have eternal life with our Savior, Jesus Christ.

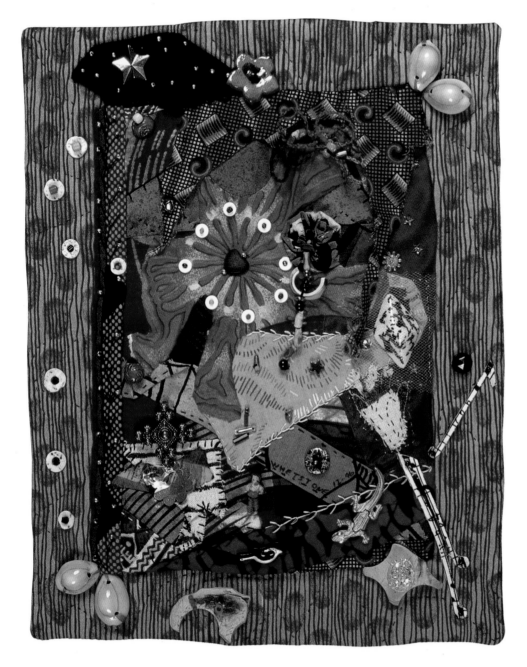

◀ RELEASED ENERGY
SHERRY WHETSTONE-McCALL

Kansas City, Missouri; 1997; cotton, pearl beads, found objects, shells; photograph by Neal Shoger

I GAINED A WHOLE NEW respect for abstract art while working on this piece. I learned that abstract art is spontaneous, but that there is a "method to the madness." "Released Energy" was born from a spiritual madness I was feeling one morning. I was compelled to create something—anything—with my hands that day. I had an eight-hour ride to Oklahoma ahead of me. This was not the time to catch up on my reading; I needed to create. Knowing this, I grabbed a handful of fabric from my scrap bag, a needle, some thread, and a pair of scissors. The first four hours of the trip, I was forced to use the scraps as they were because I had left my scissors in the back of the van! What resulted was a great lesson in creativity. Once I returned home to Kansas City, the personal objects—the "Sherry things"—were added to complete the piece. My energy had been released!

All Life Begins in Darkness ➤

Tina Brewer

Pittsburgh, Pennsylvania; 1996; 45 × 90 inches; cotton; collection of Diane Green; photograph by Fred Kenderson

LIFE IS CIRCULAR; THERE are no mistakes. Every situation is just as it should be, according to divine power. Think about a dark, dreary day and remember that the sun will inevitably shine again. Such were my thoughts in the making of this quilt. We all live and die and the universal process repeats itself. The birds in this quilt represent the seeds we plant today—like our children, who are destined to fly off tomorrow. We don't know what destiny awaits them, we don't know where the love and support we give them will land, but our hopes are with them as they begin the circle of life again.

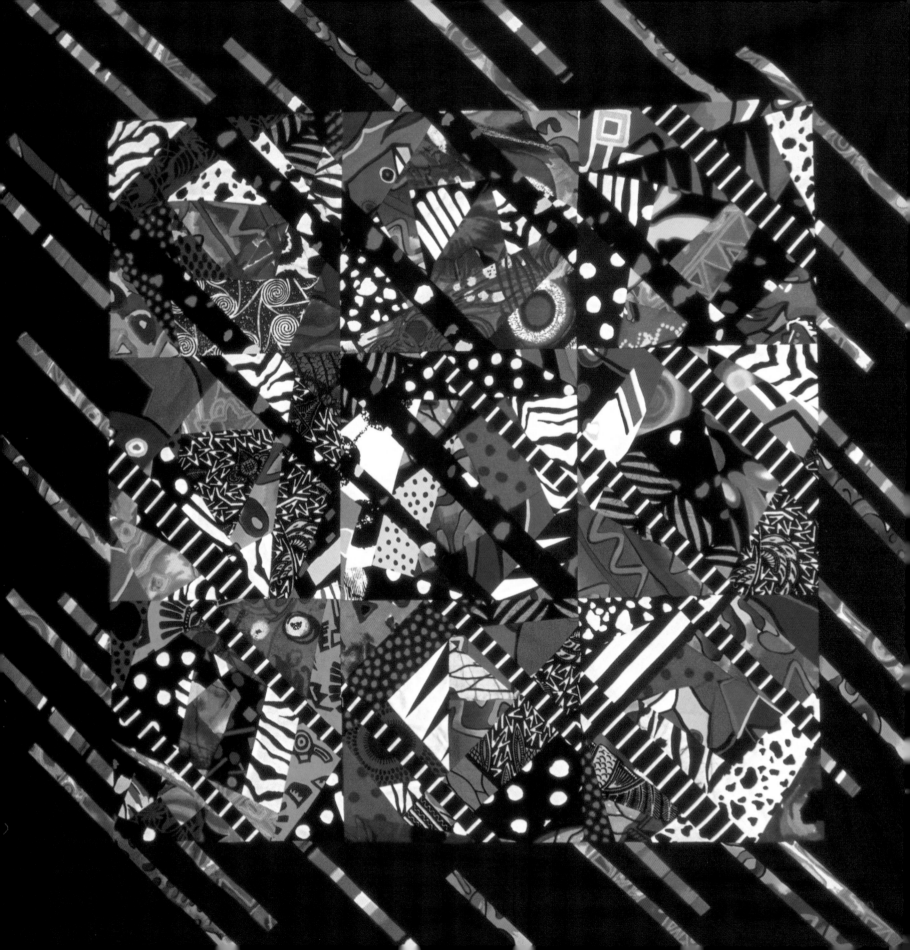

Social and Political Protest

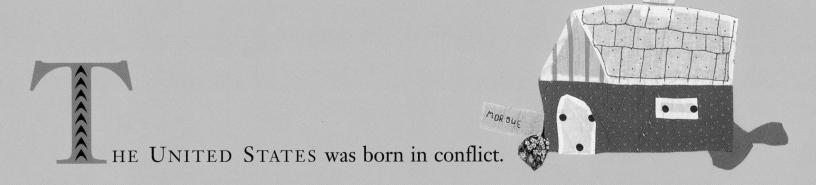

THE UNITED STATES was born in conflict.

There was the unparalleled slaughter of indigenous peoples; the strife that tore the colonies from England, their home base; and the largest forced migration in the history of mankind, which brought millions of Africans to the New World over a 200-year period. Our own history of resistance has been continuous, from mutinies by Africans on slave ships, to slave insurrec-

ABOVE: Detail from "Assassins' Bullets"

OPPOSITE: FREE SOUTH AFRICA II
SANDY BARRETT HASSAN
Washington, D.C.; 1988–94; 39 × 44 inches; all cotton, pieced; photograph by Cecile Tolliver
THIS QUILT is part of a series that was born out of my hopes for equal rights in South Africa, for a country where black people could move about freely, without the necessity of a government-issued pass. It honors the black South Africans who struggled for their freedom.

tions throughout the colonies, to the abolition, suffrage, and anti-lynching movements, and, most dramatically, to the civil rights movement of the turbulent 1960s. Because of the conditions created by slavery, racism, and Jim Crow, protest has been a defining characteristic of our literature, art, and music. Several themes run through this protest tradition: the brutality of slavery and white supremacy; the abhorrence of the portrayal of Africa and Africans as uncivilized; the hypocrisy of American democracy; the horrors of lynching; the emasculation of black men; the maligning of the character of black women; the demonization of poor blacks. ✳ Among African American women this resistance to oppression has been manifest in our activism and in our creative expression. Quilts, in particular, have provided women with outlets for their social and political concerns since the colonial era; they have been used as weapons against a range of societal injustices. Abolitionist Sarah Grimké advised women to embroider anti-slave slogans and images so that the points of their needles could "prick the slave-owner's conscience"; freed slaves made freedom quilts, and quilts were made to celebrate the passing of the first Civil Rights Act; Susan B. Anthony spoke about women's rights for the first time at a quilting bee. ✳ Contemporary African American quilts also reflect a broad range of social and political issues. There are constant reminders of the institution of slavery and the persistence of racism. Julia A. Payne's "Bondage," Betty Leacraft's "Camouflage, A Means of Survival," which deals with the plight of indigenous peoples in the Americas, Wini Akissi McQueen's "Ode to Edmund," Ruth A. Ward's "The Guiding Star," and Viola Burley-Leake's "Middle Passage" fall into this category.

ABOVE: *Detail from "Imbayerudo"*
ABOVE, RIGHT: *Detail from "Million Man March Quilt"* OPPOSITE: *Detail from "Middle Passage"*

Burley-Leake's stark black and white "Middle Passage" is as jarring as the seemingly beautiful scene in Payne's "Bondage." "The Guiding Star" by Ward subtly reminds us of the unquenchable optimism of those who used the North Star as their compass to guide them to freedom, while both McQueen's "Ode to Edmund" and Leacraft's "Camouflage" express the harsh realities of current-day African Americans, the progeny of those hopeful sojourners to freedom only a few short generations ago. ✳ Virginia Harris has chosen to make a series of quilts that address the issue of the recent burning of black churches in the Deep South. There is also concern expressed about intraracial violence, about what we are doing to each other within our own community. Zene Peer's "Graveyard Decorations" decries black-on-black crime, self-destructive behaviors such as drug use, and the devastating impact these are having on our youth. ✳ Environmental issues, particularly the problem of drift-net fishing, are dealt with in Sandra K. German's "Peaceful Lagoon." Kyra E. Hicks critiques a major cultural icon in "Black Barbie" and reminds us of the hurt caused by this figure that was "never intended for me." Anti-apartheid sentiments are expressed by African Americans who felt connected to the plight of South Africans. Aline Moyler's "Imbayerudo" and Sandy Hassan's "Free South Africa" quilts are powerful and moving statements about the evils of the white South African government. ✳ For the artists in this section, art has become a political weapon. Like African American writers, painters, and other artists, these quilters use their work to move the viewer beyond a cursory recognition of the problems they are exposing. While they critique the social and political realities of our time, they seem to be moved by an eternal optimism that says, "If I can reach one person, we can change the world."

◄ DECISIONS
EDNA J. PETTY

East St. Louis, Illinois; 1993; 67 × 45 inches; cotton, polyester, wool; collection of Missouri Historical Society, St. Louis, Missouri; photograph by David Schultz

IRONICALLY, A LACK OF inspiration inspired this piece. Everything in the news seemed depressing and negative. I tried to read only positive stories in the newspaper, yet it always seemed as if the world was in such an uproar. I remember dreaming of the power of government in all of our lives, and wondering why it couldn't use this power to make more positive and constructive decisions. In this quilt, I chose dark colors to portray my feelings of dismay, but I also added a few hints of blue for its calming effect, and tiny silver metallic threads to represent rays of hope. The red tones symbolize the bloodshed caused by others, as well as by ourselves. "Decisions" was my way of soothing my emotional frustration with the chaos in the world.

▲ CINDERELLA
KYRA E. HICKS

Kansas City, Missouri; 1995; 87 × 77 inches; cotton; photograph by Kyra E. Hicks

FAIRY TALES LIE. In this "Cinderella" quilt, the princess has been waiting for almost thirty years for her prince to arrive. The clock is about to strike thirty, instead of midnight. She is tired and has decided to be direct about her shoe size.

BLACK BARBIE ➤
KYRA E. HICKS

Kansas City, Missouri; 1996; 76 × 47 inches; cotton; photograph by Kyra E. Hicks

BARBIE, AMERICA'S DOLL, was never intended for me. I created the "Black Barbie" quilt after noticing how, in several ads for the doll, the black version was usually photographed behind the white version and rarely had a name of her own. What are we teaching our young girls?

◄ BONDAGE
JULIA A. PAYNE

Denver, Colorado; 1996; 63.5 × 63.5 inches; cotton; photograph by John Bonath ·

INTO MY QUILT I stitched the memory of the African American slave. The front of the quilt represents the institutionalization of slavery, symbolized by a slave ship, in which Africans were chained like animals in crates and brought over to the "New World." The zigzag-patterned quilting in the green border area is a common African tribal representation of eternity and the continuation of life, with its never-ending highs and lows. While working, I was asked many times by people, "Why quilt the past?" My answer to this question is that quilting the past helps me to remember where I came from and where I'm trying to go.

MIDDLE PASSAGE ➤
VIOLA BURLEY–LEAKE

Washington, D.C.; 1997; 6 × 7 feet; cotton, cotton blends; photograph by Viola Burley-Leake

THIS QUILT WAS INSPIRED by slavery, the Black Holocaust, and draws a connection between the history of Africans and African Americans. The central figures are an enraged slave man and woman touching a fully stocked slave ship as it sails through human bondage and death. Workers in sugarcane and cotton fields are also depicted. The woman with the image of the white man embedded in her head is watching the burning of a black church.

◄ PEACEFUL LAGOON
SANDRA K. GERMAN

Loveland, Ohio; 1996; 60 × 80 inches; cotton, paper, beads, metallic threads, reverse appliqué, bobbin work, machine quilted; photograph by Sandra K. German

HAVING LIVED IN New York, Hawaii, California, and Wisconsin, I have an affinity for our oceans and great waterways, along with a keen interest in their preservation. One of the practices that threatens them is drift-net fishing, which indiscriminately captures and kills everything it ensnares. "Peaceful Lagoon" pictures a seascape unspoiled by man's greed. It was created for an annual exhibition of art quilts by the Aullwood Audubon Center and Farm, where it won the 1996 Viewers' Choice award. Some very unusual materials were utilized, including Mylar gift wrap, iridescent Lycra swimwear fabric, re-embroidered lace, tulle, nylon organdy, and cotton balls. The sewing machine techniques include corded double-needle work, trapunto, beading by machine, reverse-bobbin work, embroidery, reverse appliqué, and more.

IMBAYERUDO ➤
ALINE V. MOYLER

Mt. Vernon, New York; 1993; 92 × 104 inches; cottons; photograph by Sara Wells

THIS QUILT WAS INSPIRED by the homes of the South African Ndebele tribes, who were forcibly removed from the fertile farms they had lived on for generations and relocated to the inhospitable, arid, and harsh land of the veld. Though suffering great hardships under apartheid, their indomitable spirit and creativity emerged through the startling, abstract exterior designs found on their homes. Taking certain liberties, I can imagine one of my sisters dreaming of some of the gifts of nature as she sits in front of her beautiful home: flowers, fruits, trees, rain clouds, tall grasses, mountains, moons, stars, and beautifully woven spiderwebs. When I created the blocks for this quilt, I was in a spiritual frenzy, determined to make each one uniquely different. When it was completed, a friend and her father from Zimbabwe named it "Imbayerudo," which means "house of love."

◀ GRAVEYARD DECORATIONS
ZENE PEER

Milwaukee, Wisconsin; 1993; 39.5 × 34.5 inches; cottons; photograph by Bill Simmons

THIS PIECE WAS INSPIRED, unfortunately, by a very deadly year for our youth in the city of Milwaukee. There were many killings of young black people for "little reasons," arguments over coats, careless words, and the like. It hurt me so much, and this piece was wrung from my pained spirit. The imagery and use of mixed media are meant to be at once self-explanatory and sobering for the viewer.

MILLION MAN MARCH QUILT ▶
ALINE V. MOYLER

Mount Vernon, New York; 1996; 60 × 80 inches; cotton, blends; photograph by Sara Wells

AS THE MILLION MAN MARCH approached, I decided to commemorate this historical event in a quilt so its significance would not be lost in future years. These are some of its elements: Muslims and Christians acting in concert with one another; remembering our black and brown males who through inadequate schooling and lack of jobs become a part of the prison industry; corporate as well as blue-collar workers standing shoulder to shoulder; the taking of a pledge. Only half of the Capitol is represented, because half of us believe that Washington doesn't always represent us; the pyramid represents dollars. The cowry shells are symbolic of "whatever your gifts, pass them on"; the tears of joy symbolize the camaraderie shown brother toward brother. A zippered pouch contains the mission statement as outlined by the organizers of the march. On one side of the Reflecting Pool are the spirits of those men who for whatever reason could not attend, and on the other side are the spirits of those who came before us but continue to monitor our paths.

THE COLOR OF CHRISTMAS
JULIA A. PAYNE

Denver, Colorado; 1996; 33.5 × 50 inches; cotton, paper, beads, buttons, found objects, hand quilted; photograph by John Bonath

EVER SINCE I WAS a child, I have had trouble dealing with Christmas, because it seems to me that its meaning is not really understood. People don't take the time to understand Christmas. There is too much greed, ungratefulness, loneliness, debt, and so on associated with a holiday supposedly celebrating the simple and pure joys of giving and receiving. People seem to have forgotten the real meaning of Christmas, and sometimes I wonder if they have ever known it. "The Color of Christmas" is my protest against this.

◄ HOME ALONE, TOO
WINI AKISSI MCQUEEN

Macon, Georgia; 1993; 39 × 58 inches; cotton, dyeing, photo-transfer printing, piecing, quilting; photograph by Linda Tabler

"HOME ALONE, TOO" GETS its title from the popular movie *Home Alone*. It depicts a day in the life of a young American boy who, like many other children, has the television as a baby-sitter. The quilt was inspired by my experiences with the children of the Davis Homes public housing community in Macon, Georgia. Besides introducing the children to fabric art (batiking, stamp printing, and dyeing), I explored broad topics with them, such as values, racism, nutrition—anything. One day they were eagerly making a list of their favorite TV shows; I expected to see two or three entries, but instead, many of the children had two-page lists. I decided to investigate these programs so I could better understand the images and ideas that filled their lives. For two days I sat my camera in front of the television and each hour took a photo of whatever image appeared.

⏶ The Guiding Star
Ruth A. Ward

Pittsburgh, Pennsylvania; 1995; 66.5 × 45 inches; cotton; photograph by Iris Dawn Parker

IT HAS ALWAYS AMAZED me that runaway slaves were able to use the North Star to guide them to the free North and Canada. When designing this quilt, I knew that it would have a sky and stars and people, but beyond that I had no idea how the finished piece would look. I knew that I wanted a night sky with the North Star and the Big Dipper conforming to their actual positions in the heavens. The sky dictated the size of the piece, its basic color, and the outline of the trees and the people. I overdyed fabric, machine-pieced the sky, and hand-appliquéd the trees and people. Metallic thread and star beads added the finishing touch.

◄ IN AND OUT
DOROTHY HOLDEN

*Charlottesville, Virginia; 1996; 54 × 57 inches;
cotton; photograph by Michael Bailey*

"IN AND OUT" PORTRAYS the schisms
of race in this country, a very emotional
subject for me, and it took me a year to
make the quilt. The cross in the center
represents the church, where some people justify the schism by quoting the
Bible. The figures who have transcended
racial barriers are surrounded and guided
by angel stars. The lighter figures at the
base, going toward the window, represent those who are still struggling to
overcome their own racial barriers. The
colors of the fabrics represent the elements of earth, wind, water, and fire.

AMERICAN ICONS ►
YVONNE WELLS

*Tuscaloosa, Alabama; 1995; 85 × 73 inches; cotton;
courtesy of Robert Cargo Folk Art Gallery; photograph
by Robert Cargo Folk Art Gallery*

I WAS INSPIRED TO make this quilt because I had a lot of questions. Even
though Miss Liberty and Uncle Sam are
holding the balanced scales of justice, are
they equal? When the Liberty Bell rings,
does it ring the same for all people
regardless of race, creed, or national origin? Can we say that the twelve people
on a jury are our peers?

▲ Assassins' Bullets
Yvonne Wells

Tuscaloosa, Alabama; 1990; 66 × 65 inches; cotton; courtesy of Robert Cargo Folk Art Gallery; photograph by Robert Cargo Folk Art Gallery

WHEN CERTAIN INDIVIDUALS are instrumental in advancing the civil rights of others, inevitably something happens to them. Here Abraham Lincoln, Martin Luther King, Jr., and John F. Kennedy lie on gurneys in the morgue; bullets bearing the names of their assassins are aimed at their bodies. Grave markers at the bottom have their dates of birth and dates of death. Flags are at half-staff on both sides of the quilts.

ODE TO EDMUND ➤
WINI AKISSI McQUEEN

Macon, Georgia; 1993; 62 × 39 inches; photo transfer on cotton; photograph by Lina Tabler

"ODE TO EDMUND" IS a part of my Urban Kente Literacy series, which is based on research done in the 1930s by the WPA, whose field-workers recorded personal accounts of the lives of former slaves, including their education. This particular quilt is inspired by the account of Edmund Carlisle, who had been severely brutalized because of his persistent attempts to become literate. The impetus behind this quilt series came from my efforts to understand how history influences our current predicament as black people. How was it that a people who had once designed sophisticated math systems, as illustrated in the Rhine Papyrus, could be reduced to such a low literacy status? Why are our children without a basic understanding of the importance of literacy? What I concluded, after lots of research and soul-searching, is that despite the rhetoric of liberalism and liberation, the social and political commitment toward cultivating and rehabilitating black people's literacy remains as ambivalent as it was a hundred years ago. This quilt, then, is a tribute to the Americans of African descent who have struggled, regardless of the reward/punishment system, to be true to their own intellect.

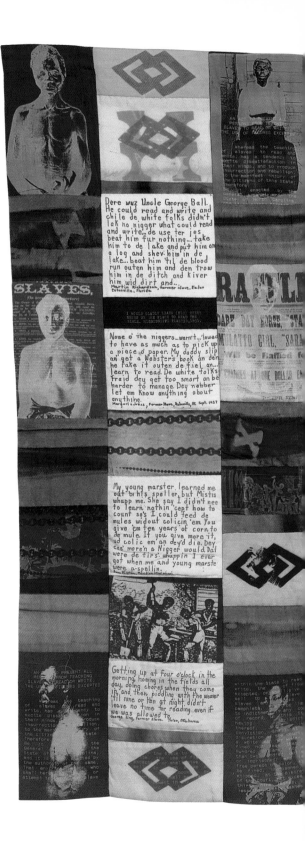

◄ CAMOUFLAGE: A MEANS OF SURVIVAL
BETTY LEACRAFT

Philadelphia, Pennsylvania; 1992; 72 × 52 inches; dyeing, photo-transfer printing, piecing, quilting; photograph by Will Brown

I DEDICATE "CAMOUFLAGE: A Means of Survival" to the memory of my African ancestors, to the ancestors of all indigenous peoples of the Americas, and to their present-day descendants. "Camouflage" explores only a few of the many survival mechanisms created by Africans in order to continue practicing their traditional spiritual beliefs and customs despite slavery and oppression. In many places throughout the African Diaspora, these cultural retentions have been passed on from one generation to the next—gifts from the ancestors to their descendants.

ONE NATION ►
VIRGINIA R. HARRIS

Albuquerque, New Mexico; 1996; 49 × 39 inches; cotton, beads, embroidery; collection of Mid-Peninsula YWCA, Palo Alto, California; photograph by Virginia R. Harris

THE ENTIRE IMAGE OF this quilt came to me after Attorney General Janet Reno's statements concerning the string of church burnings in the South. According to Reno, there was no evidence that the burnings were "racially motivated." That same statement was made about slavery, lynchings, job discrimination—on and on. The irony of using Christian symbols to perpetuate and justify racist violence has never escaped me.

The burning cross divides overt racism and covert racism. On the left members of the Ku Klux Klan stand

proud in their bedsheets watching the lynching of a black soldier. On the right side, the Klansmen are part of the background and have achieved legitimacy. The father and daughter (to show that women are as guilty of racism as men) blend with the background, standing with arms folded, a gasoline can at their feet, watching the church burn. The ribbons on the lynched soldier's chest represent some of the campaigns in which African American soldiers have been involved, from the Civil War to Vietnam to the Gulf War.

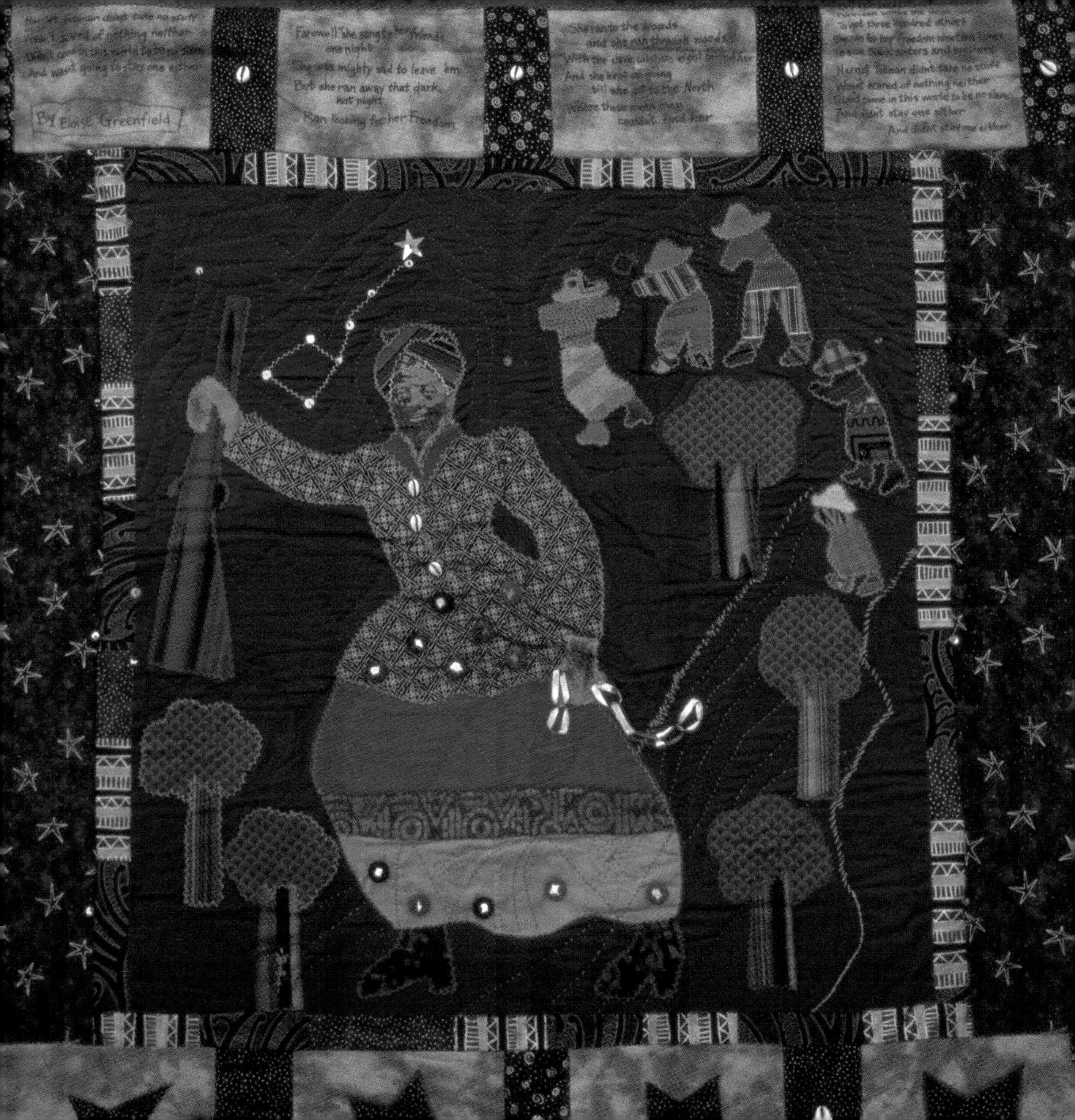

Praise Songs

ANCESTOR worship and respect for elders characterize the African cultural heritage that blacks brought with them to the New World. In a society that has not valued our humanity or recognized our accomplishments, it has been imperative that African Americans find ways to affirm their worth in a hostile land. And so "praise songs" for our heroes and heroines have played an important role

ABOVE: Detail from "Ode to Harriet Powers"

OPPOSITE: THE HARRIET TUBMAN QUILT
CHARLOTTE LEWIS
Portland, Oregon; 1996; 56 × 60 inches; cotton; collection of Makini Harris; photograph by Charlotte Lewis

"THE HARRIET TUBMAN QUILT" was created for a Kwanzaa exhibit at the Interstate Firehouse Cultural Center. The inspiration for the piece came from a poem about this brave woman. Tubman made nineteen trips to the South to bring runaway slaves through the Underground Railroad to freedom. She was responsible for the freedom of over 300 African Americans.

in our culture and appear, as well, as themes in our quilts. Activists such as Harriet Tubman, Marcus Garvey, and Martin Luther King, Jr., are remembered, as are artists and musicians. Cultural organizations such as the Dance Theatre of Harlem and the Women of Color Quilter's Network, and Afrocentric cultural traditions such as Kwanzaa are also celebrated. There are praise songs for particular family members, friendships are honored, historic events are celebrated, and cultural icons are memorialized. Praise songs enable us to affirm African American life, to counter stereotypes, and to restore our self-esteem as a people. ✳ In the quilts here, women from all walks of life are affirmed in many different ways. A former slave and famous abolitionist is the subject of "The Harriet Tubman Quilt" by Charlotte Lewis. Considered the "Moses of her people," Tubman brought more than 300 slaves north on the Underground Railroad, which had helped her escape slavery in 1849. Peggie L. Hartwell's "Ode to Harriet Powers" memorializes another ex-slave, a quilter whose two surviving narrative quilts have been preserved in the Smithsonian Institution and the Museum of Fine Arts in Boston. More generally, Nedra Bonds's "The Full Moon, The Arch, The Mississippi & 4 Women From Kansas" and Francelise Dawkins's "Ancient Mother's Visitation" honor women for their strength, power, wisdom, and life-giving force. ✳ Closer to home, family members are a major source of inspiration for quiltmakers. In her variation of the traditional quilting pattern called Rebecca's Fan, Gwendolyn Magee creates "Infinity," a birthday gift to her husband, an avid astronomy enthusiast. Jacquelyn Hughes Mooney's "Jane" celebrates the life of her great-grandmother, a for-

ABOVE: *Detail from "From the Drums Came All That Jazz"* OPPOSITE: *Detail from "Kwanzaa Quilt"*

mer slave, and her legacy of strength to subsequent generations. Joyce Scott's "Three Generations" actually includes the work of her grandmother and mother, acknowledging the legacy of creativity passed on to her by her foremothers. Carolyn W. Cameron's "Requiem" is a moving memorial to her father; inspired by her mother's desire to keep something of his close to her, the quilt incorporates a number of his ties. Brenetta Ward's "Perspectives of My Son" acknowledges her child's potential and anticipates a bright future for him. The subject of Ana Arzu Titus' "Palula's Daughter," who died of AIDS in Honduras, is now in a safe place, having been ushered there by mother spirits, and Kyra E. Hicks's quilt honors her family history with "Aunt Alzeda's Sunday Concerts." ✳ Michael Cummings's poignant and powerful "Dreams Deferred" was created to memorialize the lives of the nineteen children killed in the infamous Oklahoma City bombing. Using actual toys and children's clothing, and spending hours of "tender loving care" in the construction of this quilt, was a healing process for him as well. In his praise song for these children whose dreams have been forever deferred, he reminds us of the importance of memories in the slow process of recovery from such national trauma. ✳ On a happier note, there are the traditional American celebrations of Thanksgiving, Christmas, and New Year's, but many may not be aware of the celebrations that are unique to African Americans or the different ways in which we deal with national holidays. Kwanzaa has now become well known as a year's-end holiday celebrating the fruits of the harvest; it is a time for reflection and planning, a time to recommit to the Nguzo Saba, the seven principles of blackness as extolled by Dr. Maulana Karenga, founder of the holiday. In Roland L. Freeman's "Kwanzaa Quilt," African symbols appear on various textile items used for decoration. But while Kwanzaa has acquired a more visible, commercial profile in recent years, other days held dear by African Americans are less well known. African Americans remember staying home from school on Emancipation Day, the day Abraham Lincoln signed the Emancipation Proclamation, freeing slaves held in states at war with the Union. African Americans living in the Southwest may also remember spending a day at the amusement park to celebrate Juneteenth. This holiday commemorates the 17th of June, 1865, when those still held as slaves in Texas received the news of freedom. ✹ Despite the hardships, there has been much to celebrate in the African American experience. Africans captured and taken to America as slaves brought memories of a rich native culture, in which music served an important function as a communal activity. In the United States, blacks were the originators of spirituals, blues, and jazz. Chris Clark's "Louis Armstrong" is a praise song for one of the most influential and famous of all jazz artists; the quilt also links the improvisational techniques of jazz and quiltmaking, America's two original art forms. Similarly, Tina Brewer's "A Note to Billy" and "From the Drums Came All That Jazz" acknowledge the gift of jazz to the world. ✹ What African Americans have realized for generations is that we must celebrate who we are, what we've accomplished, and what we have given the nation and the world. Without our praise songs, it would be difficult to remember our extraordinary history.

ABOVE: *Detail from "Aunt Alzeda's Sunday Concerts"*

Robert Scott Duncanson: The Man and His Work ➤

WINI AKISSI MCQUEEN

Macon, Georgia; 1992; 63 × 42 inches; cotton, photo transfer and Van Dyke brown-printing, batik; photograph by Ken Krakow

THIS QUILT WAS COMMISSIONED by the Taft Museum in Cincinnati on the occasion of its 60th anniversary for the exhibit "Tribute to the Tafts." It is an homage to Robert S. Duncanson, a 19th-century landscape painter who was the first African American artist to receive international acclaim. The quilt border features a statement of Duncanson's personal philosophy, excerpted from one of his letters: "Love is my principle, order is the basis, progress is the end." The basic composition of the quilt is "crazy quilt" piecing, and it includes Duncanson's letters to a friend, in one of which he denies that he has rejected his racial identity. Other blocks highlight elements depicting the turbulent times in which he lived, Underground Railroad routes into Ohio, a certificate of freedom like the one Duncanson may have used during his travels around America, and images of kidnapping and forced unpaid labor. Duncanson's image appears in the center of the quilt as he was photographed by J. W. Winder in 1868, and as a distorted figure representing the physical and emotional deterioration that preceded his death.

◄ LOUIS ARMSTRONG
CHRIS CLARK

Birmingham, Alabama; 1994; 35 × 41 inches; cotton, acrylic paint; photograph by Chris Clark

THE STRIP QUILT THAT forms the background here was inspired by the improvisational nature of jazz and by the asymmetrical arrangements of cloth commonly seen in African American quilts. Louis Armstrong's use of improvisation in his playing reminds me of how I improvise when stitching together a quilt. The Armstrong quilt is the first in a series that has jazz as its theme.

PURPLE HAZE ➤
JACQUELYN HUGHES MOONEY

New Orleans, Louisiana; 1996; 65 × 75 inches; cotton; collection of Heather and Anthony Fortier; photograph by Charles Lundy

"PURPLE HAZE" WAS CREATED as an anniversary gift for the collection of Anthony and Heather Fortier and represents this couple's desire for wisdom as they continue in their married life. Purple is commonly used to represent wisdom—defined as the "practical application of knowledge"—and royalty. The "I'm hipped" appliqués, from my "Big City Woman" quilt series, shows my regard for the wisdom based in our loins, and though we often wish to remove this pronounced part of our body, we also carry life-giving stability there. I wanted to surround these regal women with silks, cottons, and brocades, to feel good for this company of sisters, and with spirals and circles to signify their never-ending power.

◄ PALULA'S DAUGHTER
ANA ARZU TITUS

New York, New York; 1996; 46 × 96 inches; cottons, machine quilted; photograph by Ernest Oliveri

PALULA'S SIXTEEN-YEAR-OLD girl, who died of AIDS, was the inspiration for this quilt. The virus found her in a remote corner of the world—Honduras. The girl never left the village, so no one knows how she got it. Everyone there was puzzled. They prayed every day for her recovery. She was treated with herbal medicines that had worked in the past, but she continued to wither away. Palula was consoled at the funeral when told her child had been taken by the ancestral mother and grandmother spirits to a safe and quiet place.

PALM TREE OF DEBORAH ➤
ADRIENE CRUZ

Portland, Oregon; 1995; 35 × 38 inches; cotton, acrylic paint, beads, shells; photograph by Keith Aden

"DEBORAH" IS THE MOST challenging work I've ever created. The project required research in unfamiliar territory, the Bible. I read the short passage about Deborah over and over again, unable to "see" her. Finally I used an old photograph of my Jamaican great-grandmother, Mabel Gurtin, as my guide. I trusted her spirit would be with me to paint the face of a wise woman with divine power. Feeling that the palm tree must also be blessed with wisdom and power, I painted fabric with preprinted faces for the front of the tree, with the eyes of the faces representing the vision of the ancestors.

◄ ODE TO HARRIET POWERS
PEGGIE L. HARTWELL

New York, New York; 1995; 46 × 50 inches; cotton, machine appliquéd and quilted; photograph by Sarah Wells

HARRIET POWERS, AN AFRICAN American woman who was born into slavery in October 1837, is famous for two Bible quilts she made. One quilt is now at the Smithsonian Institution in Washington, D.C.; the other, at the Museum of Fine Arts in Boston, Massachusetts. Powers was a very spiritual woman; her quilts reveal that about her. Through her creative genius, her quilts speak of hope and a wish for well-being. Her illustrations were of life, death, sorrow, and suffering, yet the people in the quilts represent hope, mercy, and justice. Her quilts are beautiful expressions of faith and survival, constructed out of the very substance from which she was made—sheer determination. Through narrative quiltmaking, Harriet Powers illustrated not only her religious beliefs but also stories she had heard about local legends and accounts of astronomical occurrences. This wonderful folk artist, who could not write, defied all odds by recording life on cloth, leaving behind her unique vision of the world. This quilt is an homage to her.

▲ THE FULL MOON, THE ARCH, THE MISSISSIPPI & 4 WOMEN FROM KANSAS
NEDRA BONDS

Kansas City, Kansas; 1996; 32 × 32 inches; cotton, acrylic paint; photograph by Martin Chislom

SISTERHOOD FLOWERS IN THE most unexpected places. The Association of American Cultures held its biannual conference in St. Louis in 1996. Among the participants were the four women pictured in the quilt. We had met because of a mutual interest in the arts, but we didn't get to know each other until we spent those days under the arch. Over dinner, we laughed so hard that people in the restaurant thought we were drunk. Our happiness, fueled by girl talk, rested in the commonality of our life experiences. We claimed each other as "sisters," a long way from home.

L'MERCHIE FRAZIER

Roxbury, Massachusetts; 1996; 40 × 42 inches; cotton, beads, metallic threads; photograph by L'Merchie Frazier

"FROM A BIRMINGHAM JAIL: MLK" depicts the life and work of Dr. Martin Luther King as a visual prayer. In the letter he wrote in 1957 while jailed in Birmingham, Alabama, for his stance on civil rights, he responded to the clergy, citing the need for more of what his accusers had termed "creative extremists." The quilt also displays excerpts from other speeches and events in his life. The design of the quilt recalls traditional African strip quilting and simulates "freedom" quilts, which served as clothesline maps, signposts, and coded language for the Underground Railroad, leading African American slaves to freedom. Much of the iconography of this quilt is from Egypt and Central and West Africa. The beadwork and cowry shells represent themes of fertility, wealth, prosperity, cosmic forces, and redemption. A pocket holds quilted news articles, including an account of the 1964 awarding of the Nobel Peace Prize to Dr. King.

⋀ WHIRLIGIGS AND THINGS THAT TWIST AND TURN

RUTH A. WARD

Pittsburgh, Pennsylvania; 1996; 40 × 42 inches; cotton, hand appliquéd and quilted; photograph by Dawn Parker

THIS PIECE WAS DESIGNED in response to a challenge by Natalie Joy Mays of the African American Heritage Quilter's Guild. We were challenged to make a wall quilt with units no more than four inches square that also included the four challenge fabrics. I can truly say that this piece quilted itself, going through several changes as I tried to find various patterns and designs to complete it. Our lives are made up of magic circles, each one a sacred place connected to our personal lives. And all life, however fragile or fragmented, is linked to the universal circle, of which we are all a part.

◄ REQUIEM
CAROLYN W. CAMERON

Kansas City, Kansas; 1991; 36 × 36 inches, cottons; collection of Fern Webster; photograph by Carolyn W. Cameron

MY FATHER, A GENTLE, scholarly man, died in 1988. We shared a passion for books, anthropology, classical music and jazz, travel, and heated discussions around the dinner table. After my dad died, my mother requested that I create a fabric piece for her, using my father's ties. It was not something I wanted to do, but Mother's request didn't entirely leave my mind, and after two years, I began to think about the ties and what I could do with them. "Requiem" is a memorial, created from the memories of the love my father shared with many people. "Requiem" also honors the many ways my father was important to me, and to the many lives he touched as an early proponent of equality and civil rights; his role as a teacher to students of all ages; his enthusiasm and appreciation for all peoples; his never-ending quest for knowledge and education; and all that he gave to the community of Kansas City.

ANCIENT MOTHER'S VISITATION ►
FRANCELISE DAWKINS

Glens Falls, New York; 1995; silk, cotton, velvet, metallic threads; photograph by David Dawkins

EDWIGE DANTICAT'S MOVING BOOK *Breath, Eyes, Memories* gave birth to this highly charged piece depicting an elder, whose symbolic pregnancy makes visible to us the gift of her past, present, and future legacy. She silently stands by us until we acknowledge the loving presence of all the Mothers from whom we came.

◀ INFINITY
GWENDOLYN A. MAGEE

Jackson, Mississippi; 1995; 105.5 × 90 inches; cotton; collection of Geraldine K. Brookins; photograph by Erol Dillon

THIS QUILT IS MY modification of a traditional pattern called Rebecca's Fan. It was created as a birthday gift for my husband, D. E. Magee, Jr., who is an avid astronomy enthusiast. The name is derived from the feelings that are evoked in me whenever I look at this quilt, because the design draws me into it endlessly, almost hypnotically. It's like the dimensions of space and time that so fascinate my husband.

A NOTE TO BILLY ▶
TINA BREWER

Pittsburgh, Pennsylvania; 1994; 28 × 36 inches; collection of estate of Billy Strayhorn, Gregory A. Morris, executor; photograph by Fred Kenderson

INSPIRED BY AND IN memory of the jazz master and Pittsburgh native Billy Strayhorn, this quilt exudes the music of "Passion Flower," "Day Dream," and "Lush Life," to name a few of his compositions. Strayhorn was an intellectual and a dandy, but he was also low-key and humble. Perhaps this accounts for his giving over his talents and music to Duke Ellington. But Strayhorn was simply "happy to be in the circle of many master musicians," and this quilt represents his selflessness through floating circles of half light and half dark. The quilt also has layers of family memorabilia, celebrations, flowers, and holidays, reflecting the richness of Strayhorn's life and his many contributions to music.

◄ STAR LINE
HAZEL RODNEY BLACKMAN

Bronx, New York, 1991; 74 × 82 inches; cotton,
acrylic paint; photograph by Carolyn L. Mazloomi

THIS QUILT IS DEDICATED to Marcus Garvey. Marcus Garvey started the "back to Africa" movement, and my parents were very fond of him. The Black Star Line was to transport black Americans back to their Motherland, and Garvey sold shares in the venture. My grandfather purchased $100 in shares for his grandchildren.

LIFT EVERY VOICE AND SING ➤
ROLAND L. FREEMAN

Washington, D.C.; 1991; 67 × 67 inches; cotton;
photograph by Roland Freeman

"LIFT EVERY VOICE AND SING," the African American anthem adapted from the poem by James Weldon Johnson, inspired this quilt of the same name. The song's three stanzas accompany the drawings in the blocks. The quilt was pieced by Viola Canady and quilted by Gertrude Braan, Vivian Hoban, and Joyce Nixon, members of the Daughters of Dorcas and Sons, Washington, D.C.

◄ THREE GENERATIONS
JOYCE SCOTT

Baltimore, Maryland; 1980s; 72 × 72 inches; cotton blends, beads, shells, ribbon; photograph by Kanj Takeno

THIS QUILT WAS MADE by three generations of my family. The bottom was made by my paternal grandmother; the middle by my mother, Elizabeth; the top portion by me. The layers symbolize the ancestral link between generations of creativity. All the women in my family are very creative individuals, whose artistic talents were born out of their life experiences and self-knowledge. This quilt celebrates their ability to transcend difficult barriers and place themselves at the center of human experience, art, and consciousness.

JANE ➤
JACQUELYN HUGHES MOONEY

New Orleans, Louisiana; 1996; 60 × 68 inches; cottons; photograph by Charles Lundy

THIS QUILT CELEBRATES THE life of my great-grandmother, who worked in the "big house" on the plantation of President Zachary Taylor. I have been researching my family history and found that Great-grandmother Jane was an extraordinary woman. I am thankful for the strength that she passed on to the women in my family.

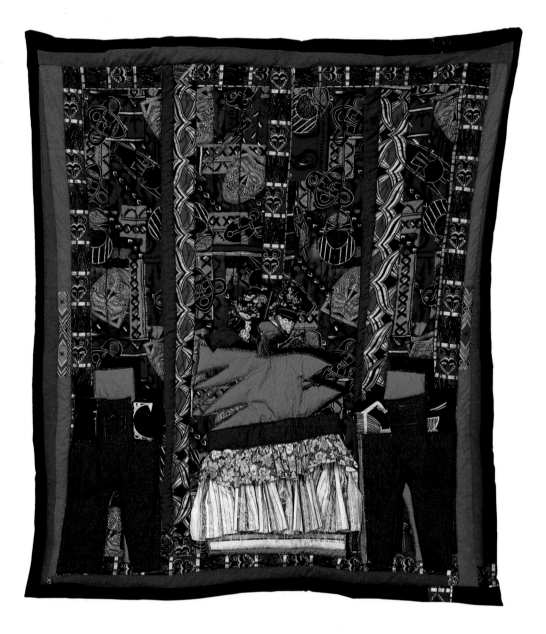

◄ TABLEAU—THE HARLEM
DANCE THEATRE
*WOMEN OF COLOR QUILTER'S
NETWORK*

*New York City chapter; 1993; 14 × 10 feet; silk,
buttons, beads, taffeta, sequins, lace, hand appliquéd,
hand quilted; photograph by Theobald Wilson*

IN CELEBRATION OF THEIR twenty-fifth
anniversary, the Dance Theatre of Harlem commissioned the New York City
chapter of the Women of Color Quilter's
Network to create a unique dance quilt.
Construction of "Tableau" began in
October 1992 and features seven of the
dance company's signature works: *Fire-
bird, Dougla, Forces of Rhythm, A Streetcar
Named Desire, Giselle, Medea,* and *A Song
for Dead Warriors.* The quilt was unveiled
at Lincoln Center's New York State The-
ater on opening night, March 16, 1993.
The quilt was designed by Marie Wilson.
The quilters in the group were Valerie J.
Bailey, June Bridgeforth, Hazel Black-
man, Yvette Walton, Mary Ellen Webb,
Marie Wilson, Peggie Hartwell, Mauline
Powell, and Marguerite Hatfield.

◄ HONEY BEES, BUTTERMILK, AND BLUES
SANDRA K. GERMAN

Loveland, Ohio; 1993; 130 × 130 inches; cottons; photograph by Linda Tabler

I MADE THE HONEY BEE blocks for a monthly guild activity. Members were instructed to use only certain "proper" colors and hand techniques—in defiance, I used neither. It was inevitable that my creative spirit would completely rebel, and I soon left the guild. This quilt is a reflection of that bittersweet association. The Rising Sun border symbolizes hopes for the future. This quilt is dedicated to the Women of Color Quilter's Network—with gratitude. Without the Network, I would feel vulnerable to the forces of convention, a "stranger in a strange land." The network ensures that diversity in quiltmaking is valued, encouraged, and preserved.

AUNT ALZEDA'S SUNDAY CONCERTS ➤
KYRA E. HICKS

Kansas City, Missouri; 1996; 88 × 70 inches; cottons, lace, photo transfers, buttons, paints; photograph by David Smalls

ALZEDA CROCKETT HACKER (b. 1907) is a passionate educator and musician, and her strong faith in God is a continual source of guidance. This indomitable matriarch of three generations prays daily for her family and community. The sheet music on the piano is James Weldon Johnson's "Lift Every Voice and Sing," which is one of Aunt Alzeda's favorites. When she plays it for the family, she insists that we sing every verse! The wall hanging above the piano is sim-

ilar to the one in Aunt Alzeda's home. It's informally called "The Fortune Teller" and features a black woman being told her fortune by a gypsy. The painting once belonged to Aunt Alzeda's great-grandmother.

▲ Kwanzaa Quilt
Roland L. Freeman

Washington, D.C.; 1989; 82 × 93 inches; cotton, hand quilted; photograph by Roland L. Freeman

I designed, chose the fabric, and hand-pieced this quilt myself. It was hand quilted by Hystercine Rankin, winner of the 1997 NEA's National Heritage Award. The quilt was made in honor of the African American holiday Kwanzaa.

That's What Friends Are For ➤
Mary Bedford Brewer

Palmdale, California; 1989–94; 78 × 108 inches; cotton, hand quilted; photograph by Pat and Tony Baguley

This quilt was made collectively in 1989 and 1990 from block exchanges of the 8 Hands Around mini-quilt group. The outer borders were designed to use a piece of every Christmas fabric in my twenty-year collection. Although the quilt was put together and taken apart three times, many happy memories are revived each time it is displayed.

◀ PERSPECTIVES OF MY SON
BRENETTA WARD

Seattle, Washington; 1996; 49 × 64 inches; cottons; photograph by Mark Ward

I DESIGNED "PERSPECTIVES" as a gift for my teenage son, Marcus. I wanted him to have a quilt that celebrated his transition from a child to a young man. I chose a modified Log Cabin pattern, using vibrant African textiles. The inner section of each block represents a unique aspect of my son's personality or heritage. Together the blocks symbolize his potential to choose what he achieves and who he becomes.

16 FEET OF DANCE ▶
FRANCES HARE

Rochester, New York; 1996; 69 × 56 inches; cotton, beads, shells; photograph by Dan Neuberber

Each foot is a part of a dance
stepping in, stepping out
flat, ball, jump.

In place, in time
off phrase, but centered.

With energy, with passion.
Forever dancing.

◄ DREAMS DEFERRED
MICHAEL CUMMINGS

New York, New York; 1997; 68 × 87 inches; cottons, beads, found objects, appliqué, machine quilted; photograph by Michael Cummings

THE TITLE OF THIS PIECE was taken from a poem of the same name by Langston Hughes, in which he asks, "What happens to a dream deferred?" In creating my quilt, I chose to commemorate the lives of the nineteen children killed in the Oklahoma City bombing incident. By carefully selecting these images and found objects, I hoped to create a visual poem of the experiences that could have nurtured and shaped their "dreams deferred."

FROM THE DRUMS CAME ALL THAT JAZZ ►
TINA BREWER

Pittsburgh, Pennsylvania; 1991; 72 × 72 inches; cotton, appliqué; photograph by Fred Kenderson

JAZZ, A SIGNIFICANT PART of the African American tradition, is one of the most precious gifts given to America. There is a sense of free-flowing energy to this quilt—movement, glory, vibrancy, manipulation of color and design, and rhythmic patterns—all of which conjures up the music of our ancestors. Can you hear the beat? Can you hear the drums telling us to embrace, protect, and preserve that which is ours?

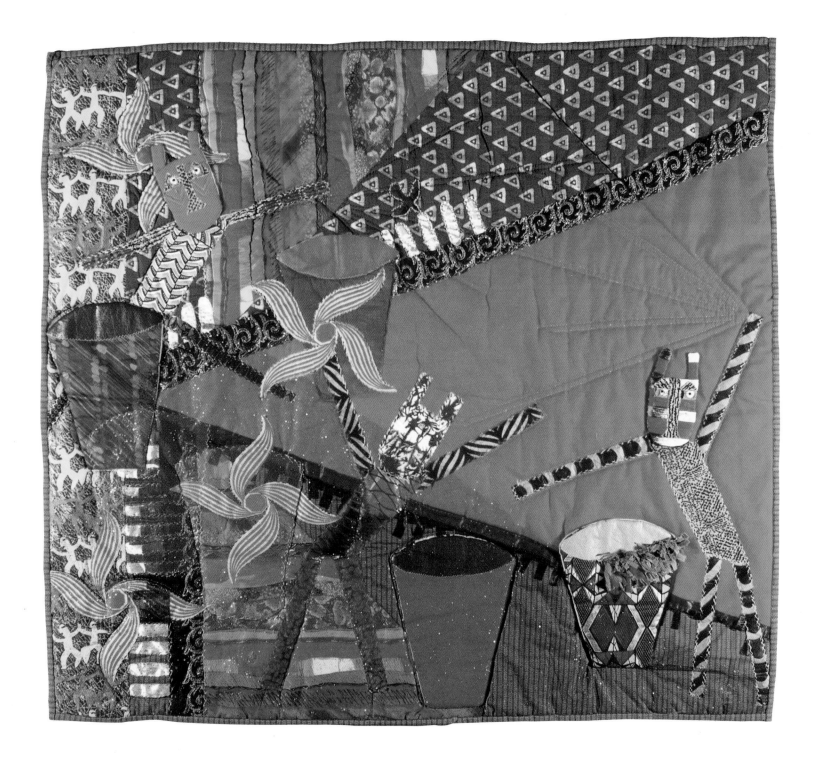

Black, Female, and Empowered

T HE TWO most important events in

contemporary American history—the civil

rights movement and the women's movement—were

distinctly significant to African American women.

Because of the rampant sexism of the black movement

and the equally strong racism in the women's move-

ment, a black women's liberation movement emerged

in the 1970s whose primary goal was to call attention

ABOVE: Detail from "Three Women"

OPPOSITE: REPRISE
MARIE WILSON
Brooklyn, New York; 1979; 5 × 5 feet; cotton; photograph by Theobald Wilson

"REPRISE" IS THE ANSWER to my own question, "What is a woman?" Silhouettes indicate the generic roles into which society insists we must fit. Please note that I was realistic enough to include an angel *and* a witch. The images of actual women celebrate many achievements. I confess that my favorite is Gertrude Benham, a glorious eccentric. She was a 19th-century explorer who spent thirty years walking around the world. She was the first woman to climb Mt. Kilimanjaro. Throughout her travels, she carried her Bible, her knitting, and her pocket Shakespeare.

to the unique situation of African American women. ✳ The 1970s also witnessed the emergence of a women's art movement, with women artists protesting their exclusion from museums, exhibitions, and art history scholarship. They

challenged the patriarchal definitions of art itself, which had marginalized much of women's creative work because it did not conform to traditional notions of fine art. One goal of the movement was to establish quiltmaking as an important art form, worthy of display in museums and of serious scholarly commentary and interpretation. ✳ This struggle for inclusion is still being waged at museums and galleries across the country, and each exhibit, scholarly presentation, paper, or book that

confirms quilting as fine art is a battle won in that war. In 1971 an exhibition by Jonathan Holstein at the Whitney Museum, entitled "Quilts As Abstract Art," took quilts off the bed and displayed them on walls. For the first time, the mainstream art world was forced to consider the artistry of quilts. ✳ Two years later Pat Mainardi wrote a classic essay, "Quilts: The Great American Art," in which she argued that quiltmaking was an empowering activity for women individually and collectively, and that it had been for generations their major creative outlet. The quilting bee was a bonding experience for women, during which they cemented friendships, exchanged ideas, told stories, and shared secrets. As gallery owner Bernice Steinbaum wrote in an essay on contemporary American quilts, quiltings bees may in fact have been "the first feminist consciousness raising group." For slave women in particular, they were festive occasions that

ABOVE: *Detail from "Joy"* OPPOSITE: *Detail from "Single Black Female"*

allowed them to escape from fieldwork and achieve a sense of community. ✳ A major theme in the quilts of contemporary black women is black womanhood: what does it mean to be an African American female in the modern era? A broad range of women's issues provides the subject matter for a number of their quilts as well. In this section one is struck, first of all, by the frequency with which black women appear as primary subjects. Sometimes portrayed as African women, in African garb, in African villages, this depiction is a way of affirming our cultural heritage and our rejection of white conceptions of black womanhood. ✳ In a culture that devalues black womanhood and defines her as ugly, it is important for black women to affirm their worth and beauty. It is noteworthy that black women, perhaps more than any other group in American society, look to themselves to define their worth, a tradition that was passed on from our slave ancestors, generation to generation. For years, black women have set their own fashion trends and determined their own beauty standards; they have also had far more positive and accepting body images than have white women. This intracultural positive reinforcement has sustained and strengthened us for generations, even in the face of constant negative portrayals of black women in general. ✳ Issues facing women in the 1990s are dealt with in this chapter, often with humor, as in Kyra E. Hicks's "Single Black Female," which captures the frustration that many single black women feel about not having a male companion. With their clear feminist messages, Marie Wilson's monumental "Reprise" and "Synonyms" are not confined to the African American experience. They celebrate the lives of women globally and point out the limitations of any narrowly conceived role for women. "Reprise" presents twelve women of unique achievement. They include women in professions we associate with men—a physicist, an astronomer, an anthropologist, an outlaw, and a gloriously eccentric explorer. "Synonyms" underscores the similarities in the lives of women despite their different cultural contexts; Western, including Native American, and Asian women are paired in similar situations, and the central image underscores the connection among women that quiltmaking provides. ✳ Certainly the second-wave women's movement resulted in an outpouring of quilts addressing issues of particular concern to women. Contemporary black quiltmakers have made important statements about the nature of womanhood and have expressed both the joys and difficulties of what it means to be black and female. Their works express the poignancy of being devalued as human beings in a value-conscious society. Yet these artists also capture in their quilts the beauty, resilience, and versatility of black women, qualities that remind us of who we are and "how we got over."

ABOVE AND RIGHT: *Details from "Yo Bloodline"*

▲ Baggett's Fragile World
SHERRY WHETSTONE-McCALL

Kansas City, Missouri; 1993; 48 × 54 inches; lace, cotton, beads, found objects; photograph by Neal Shoger

THE VICTORIAN ERA WAS one of femininity and elegance. This quilt, one of the largest pieces I have completed, was named after a friend of mine, who suggested I create "something Victorian." I enjoyed adding the sewing implements under the lamp and using different textures of fabric, like a velvet dress, lace curtains, sheer fabric for the window, and suede for the dog. The model for this piece, Gerry Sue Humphrey, truly lives as a Victorian woman would live—elegantly and with much class.

▲ I Believe I Can Fly
SHARON KERRY-HARLAN

Wauwatosa, Wisconsin; 1996; 26.5 × 22.5 inches; cotton, beads, buttons, found objects; photograph by Larry Sanders

THE MYTH THAT AFRICAN Americans could once fly has survived as a tradition in American folk culture. The debate over our ability to change our circumstances provides the main idea of this quilt. Can we rise above personal weaknesses and disadvantages, or are we stuck? This piece celebrates the viewpoint of African American women who believe in their ability to rise above adversity.

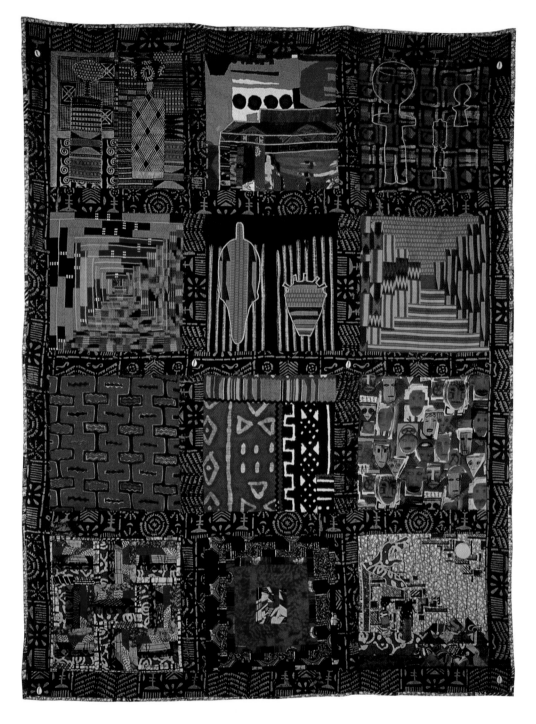

◀ JOY
DONNETTE A. COOPER

Hyattsville, Maryland; 1991; 85 × 65 inches; cottons; photograph by Donnette A. Cooper

THIS QUILT REPRESENTS MY first serious foray into quiltmaking. It was made as a Christmas gift for my sister, Carolyn Joy Cooper. I included scraps from my sister's garments and fabrics we bought together on trips to Africa. The bottom right square evokes the title of the quilt. It represents me and my sister at Hellshire Beach, Jamaica, a favorite Kingston resort for local tourists. The quilt remains in my possession, as my sister has generously refused to deprive me of my first effort.

YO BLOODLINE ▶
TINA BREWER

Pittsburgh, Pennsylvania; 1990; 45 × 72 inches; cottons; photograph by Sam Newberry

THERE WAS A TIME when man respected and harmonized with his environment and its inhabitants. Then there were wars of separation. As one's eyes move up this quilt, there are visions of the different wars suffered by those of African descent. Represented on the cloth are symbols of beasts, African tribal fights, civil and modern wars. Yo Boys are the modern-day warriors, and drugs are their weapons. Throughout the entire quilt and stemming from its central element is a line of sequins representing African American women holding up the tree of life, supporting and seeking to protect the bloodline, the Yo Boys.

Guess Who's Coming to Dinner ➤

Barbara Pietila

Baltimore, Maryland; 1993; 28 × 36 inches, cottons; photograph by Barbara Pietila

FOR MANY YEARS I thought that I was the only woman in America who had started a family without knowing how to cook. As I have grown older, I've discovered I was wrong. The days when women were required to be well versed in domestic skills are long gone. My mother was an excellent cook, and since we lived in the same household when my children were small, I had no need to learn. When she passed away, I found myself confronted with three hungry children waiting for me to prepare the tons of stuff they insisted upon eating. In time I learned to cook, but my heart goes out to those who can't and must, and especially to those, like myself, who really don't want to and must.

TRANSFORMATION ❯
ADRIENE CRUZ

Portland, Oregon; 1992; 47 × 51 inches; cotton, beads, shells; photograph by David Martinez

THIS QUILT IS VERY special to me because it is my first attempt at quilting. I'd been a tapestry crochet artist for many years and had stopped designing and exhibiting after my two daughters were born. I was unable to balance being an artist and a mother, so after much frustration, I decided to focus on what was most important, mothering. But when my youngest was three, I decided to "get a life." I was bored and boring. So I took a contemporary quilting class. It was wonderful being creative, inspired by colors again. Two classes after I started, I went to see Edjohnetta Miller's "Spirit of the Cloth" exhibit. Well, that did it. When I saw what was possible with quilting, I knew I was on the path of a whole new world as an artist, and somehow it was easier to balance quilting with my life as a mother. As I was working on this quilt, I kept hearing a voice saying, "Adriene, you just change partners and dance."

⋀ SYNONYMS
MARIE WILSON

Brooklyn, New York; 1990; 84 × 98 inches; cotton, beads, blends, lamé; buttons; photograph by Theobald Wilson

"SYNONYMS" GREW OUT OF my feeling that women's lives are very similar in every culture. I chose examples from the Western world and Asia. There are images of women celebrating their children. For example, in Japan there is a November festival called "Schischi Go San." On this day, girls of seven, boys of five, and three-year-olds of both sexes are dressed in traditional finery and taken to visit local shrines to be photographed. In New Mexico, during July the Mescalero Apache celebrate a four-day puberty ceremony in which the parents ritually present to the public their daughters who have entered womanhood. I also included images of women working at home, at the office, and in the field. The brides represent women whose relationships have led to commitment. Madame Butterfly and Billie Holiday represent disillusioned women. The central image represents the communion women can find in quilting together.

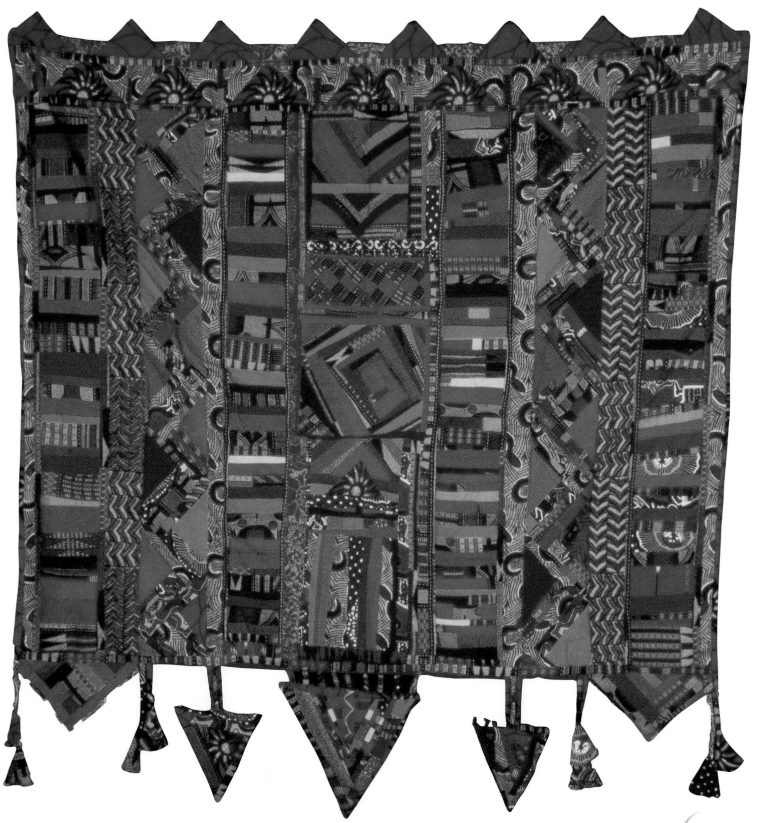

◀ Bikini Beach

Sandra Smith

Silver Spring, Maryland; 1992; 58 × 59 inches; cotton, silk, metallic thread; photograph by David Caras

"Bikini Beach" was inspired by the many happy moments my dearest friend and I have shared. The fabrics I used symbolize the activities we enjoy: eating out, fishing, and camping.

Woman ❯

Cathleen R. Bailey

Pittsburgh, Pennsylvania; 1995; cotton, paper, found objects; 21.5 × 21.5 inches; photograph by Frank Floyd Hightower

One day, as Sug Avery says in *The Color Purple*, when I was feeling poorly, I locked myself in my sewing room in order to do something creative with all those swirling emotions. The result is this piece, made mostly from panties and lingerie I bought from Goodwill. There are photos of my four daughters and two of my granddaughters; a sexy drawing of a woman by my granddaughter; pictures of women's breasts; feet and faces from *Essence* magazine. At the bottom over the word "Woman" is a photo of my legs and my disjointed face. Right above that is "The Change," and a passage that I tore out of *Essence:* "Menopause is a process. It is a season of late-summer ripeness, earth time, the time of true balance. I must say it sure sounds like freedom to me." Unfortunately, I don't know who wrote this. Going through the middle of the quilt from bottom to top are letters in red glitter: P . . . U . . . S . . . S . . . Y. No one ever notices them.

◄ SINGLE BLACK FEMALE
KYRA E. HICKS

Kansas City, Missouri; 1994; 88 × 72 inches; cotton;
photograph by David Smalls

AS AN UNMARRIED WOMAN with many unmarried women friends all crying the same blues, I designed the "Single Black Female" quilt as our song. The quilt expresses a longing not unlike those seen in newspaper personal ads, of folks seeking a relationship with a kindred spirit. When one looks closely at the quilt draped over the stool, one can see that many of the fabric pieces feature couples—a woman and cowboy, two bears sharing an umbrella, a lion and lioness, fish and water, a couple kissing—to carry the relationship theme throughout the piece. The beige background fabric has architectural drawings of houses and floor plans to suggest a deeper need for home.

THREE WOMEN ►
JULIANNE MCADOO

Pittsburgh, Pennsylvania; 1995; 27 × 29 inches;
cotton; photograph by Julianne McAdoo

"THREE WOMEN" WAS INSPIRED by the works of the renowned African American artist Romare Bearden and his method of collage. This quilt is dedicated to African American women whose voices are strong, yet vulnerable; proud, yet humble; speaking, yet listening. Many of the fabrics in this piece have been cut apart and sewn back together to give an added dimension to the surface. Since completing this quilt, I have continued to explore the technique of collage quiltmaking.

The Gallery

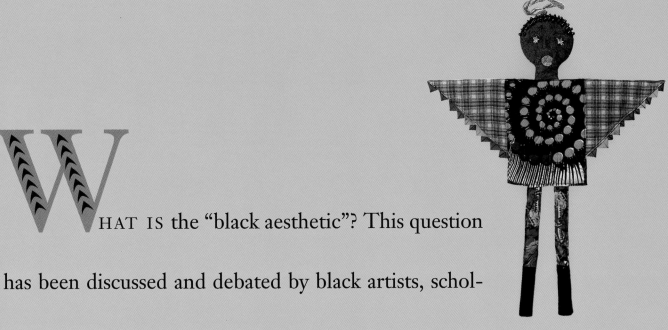

WHAT IS the "black aesthetic"? This question has been discussed and debated by black artists, scholars, and laypeople in every discipline. Part of the challenge inherent in the question lies in deciding who can or should answer it. The quarrel among blacks during the expansive era of the 1960s had everything to do with whose definition of black aesthetics was valid. Some scholars and activists believed that black art

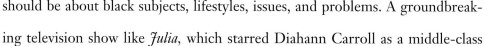

should be about black subjects, lifestyles, issues, and problems. A groundbreaking television show like *Julia*, which starred Diahann Carroll as a middle-class single parent, was thought by some to be irrelevant because the show did not challenge the status quo. By simply representing Middle America, *Julia* was criticized for not being "black" enough, despite the fact that the show offered the first black female character in her own situation comedy on prime-time national television. ✳ On the one hand, blacks often complain about the use of stereotypical representations of African Americans. On the other hand, those artists who break the mold and use a full range of expression for their art are often criticized for leaving behind their cultural identity. Adding another level of complexity to the issue of "black aesthetics" is the question of whose definition of blackness is authentic. Some of the same '60s activists who suggested that black art must be "revolutionary" were themselves academics fairly removed from the community they claimed to represent. ✳ As with many other black artists, the quilters in this section refuse to be narrowly defined. Instead they challenge common assumptions of what an African American quilt is and what it looks like. They question whether any particular subject matter or approach defines African American art, other than the ethnicity of its creator. How, for example, is abstract art by African Americans to be defined, when the black aesthetic is generally seen as figurative? Such questions regarding aesthetics can stimulate healthy debate; it is important, however, not to create new definitions that inhibit creativity. Freedom of expression is the greatest gift artists give to the world. Quilt artists, like all other artists, must be allowed that freedom. ✳ The aesthetic legacy of African American women has

ABOVE: *Detail from "Candy Box"*
OPPOSITE: *Detail from "Pueblo Pictographs"*

been grossly ignored by mainstream chroniclers of women's art. And black women artists have also been excluded from the histories of the Harlem Renaissance and the Black Arts movement of the 1960s. Though considerable attention has been given to the utilitarian nature of black women's quiltmaking, much less has been written about the artistry of their works and the ways in which their aesthetic needs are fulfilled through the process of quilting. Iconographically complex and technically excellent, the quilts in this section were designed with aesthetics as their primary impulse. They may appear to be devoid of an African American presence, except for those with African fabrics, because there are few explicitly racial images. ✳ Despite a proliferation of commentary on the "art quilt," which frequently excludes black women quiltmakers, I have avoided categorizing the pieces in this section as "art quilts" because I believe all quilts are art. There is deliberate experimentation here with format, color, and techniques, and resistance, in some cases, to the established traditions of quiltmaking. More rules are broken; new methods are invented; the essence of the "artistic" is fully expanded. ✳ These quiltmakers have indeed challenged themselves and the viewer to see how far the concepts of color, hue, and tone can be stretched. Their pieces are some of the most challenging, beautiful, and expressive examples of quilt art today. Though they may not fit the mold some may expect for African American quilts, they are, in fact, important pieces that deserve to be included. They also force us to rethink the very notion of African American quilts and to experience anew the vibrancy, originality, and passion of black artists.

Spirits of the Cloth

◀ KALEIDOSCOPE
RUTH A. WARD

Pittsburgh, Pennsylvania; 1994; 27-inch diameter; cottons, pieced; photograph by Dawn Parker

THIS IS A CHALLENGE QUILT that began with many pieces of varying shapes and color. Initially I had no idea where to start because when I looked at the pieces, I saw only confusion and disorder. The quilt pieces made me think about life, particularly our capacity to create order out of chaos. So I began to precisely piece each shape to formulate a design that, like the human spirit, is resilient, complex, and beautiful.

IN THE SPIRIT ➤
CAROLE HARRIS

Detroit, Michigan; 69 ¹/₂ × 71 inches; cotton, machine quilted; photograph by Bill Saunders

I USUALLY START OUT with something in mind—a sketch or an idea. As I play or work in a very intuitive, spontaneous way, other ideas and motifs begin to develop. In the interplay between the work and me, I let the work take over and lead me wherever it wants to go. I think that part of my being in control is being free to let the piece go where it wants to go. I like the feel of fabric, with its various textures, and I can accomplish the same end with it as with paint.

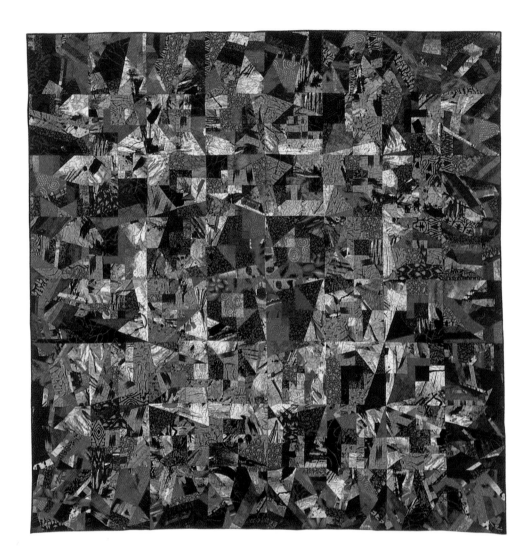

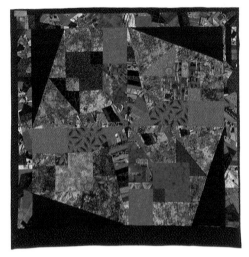

◄ ∧ THE WILD THANG
SANDRA SMITH

Silver Spring, Maryland; 1992; 64 × 64 inches;
cotton lamé, silk; photograph by David Caras

THIS QUILT, SHOWN HERE from the front
as well as the back, was an experiment in
transparency and crazy-quilting. All of
the squares in the center of the quilt are
the same design. The quilt is reversible,
with a similar design on the back.

BURGOYNE SURROUNDED ➤
KENNETH H. ROPER

Castle Rock, Colorado; 1995; 100 × 83 inches;
cottons, hand quilted; photograph by John Bonath

I LIKE MAKING QUILT patterns that have
simple lines but still provide a beautiful
and functional piece when it is done. My
grandmother Hessie would not make a
quilt without the intent of using it, and
neither do I. "Burgoyne Surrounded"
struck me as meeting those requirements.
Another reason I selected it was that my
wife "dared" me. I'm just a sucker for
challenges from beautiful women.

◀ CANDY BOX
VIRGINIA R. HARRIS

Albuquerque, New Mexico; 1994; 76 × 76 inches; cotton, machine pieced and quilted, batting; photograph by Virginia R. Harris

A JAPANESE AMERICAN FRIEND invited me to fold origami with her. Folding the papers into various objects was intriguing. What shape would result when the papers were unfolded? I cut sixteen-inch squares of freezer paper—folded, unfolded—and a fascinating new source for quilt blocks evolved. The distinct blocks disappeared as the quilt formed, and an overall pattern evolved. In an adaptation of an unfolded origami candy box, the Japanese print fabrics are grouped like pieces of candy in a box, with the special one-of-a-kind piece in the center.

STARBURST ▶
GWENDOLYN A. MAGEE

Jackson, Mississippi; 1995; 45.5 × 45.5 inches; cotton, pieced, hand quilted; collection of Geraldine K. Brookins; photograph by Erol Dillon

A CLOSE FRIEND, Geraldine Kearse Brookins, has been a great admirer of my quilts from the very beginning and hinted over the years, not too subtly, about how much she valued my work. She has exquisite taste and so I am very flattered. This quilt was made for her as a Christmas gift. It is based on the Broadway Star pattern and was my exploration into the use of earth tones. A different design is quilted in the center of each star.

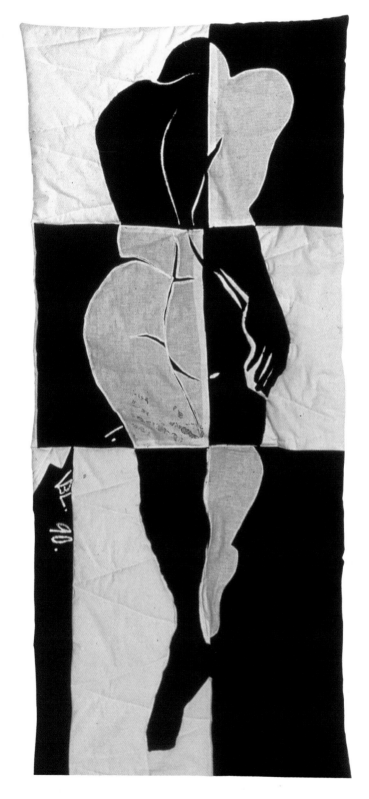

◄ HE
VIOLA BURLEY-LEAKE

Washington, D.C.; 1990; 25 × 62 inches; cotton and synthetics; photograph by Viola Burley-Leake

THE INSPIRATION HERE WAS a sleeping male figure with good muscle mass and form. I wanted to study the sleeping figure in its simplicity of presentation, color, mass, and form. This quilt was a study for at least four other quilts entitled "Dream Series."

WHICH WINDOW IS YOURS? ►
JANET WATERS BAILEY

Baltimore, Maryland; 1996; 26 × 34 inches; cotton, hand quilted; photograph by Isaac Jones

WHEN I STARTED THIS quilt, there was no final vision for the work, just an idea for a new way to assemble pieces of fabric. By the time the quilt top was in the first stages of piecing, I saw old memories of millions and millions of New York high-rise apartment buildings.

‹ ∧ JEWEL FIRE
GWENDOLYN A. MAGEE

Jackson, Mississippi; 1996; 108 × 88.5 inches; cottons, pieced, hand quilted; photograph by Erol Dillon

RAINBOWS, OR ANYTHING ELSE that incorporates movement and color, have always held me spellbound. I have long wanted to duplicate this effect. "Jewel Fire," shown here from the front as well as the back, is my first attempt and uses a traditional quilt block—Endless Chain—as its base.

LUSH LIFE ›
CAROLE HARRIS

Detroit, Michigan; 1994; 26 × 34 inches; cotton, machine quilted; photograph by Bill Saunders

IN THE INTERPLAY between the work and me, I let the work take me wherever it wants to go. I like the feel of the fabric here, its various textures, and I can accomplish the same end with it as with paint.

∧ Mr. and Mrs. Afro P. Angel and Michael
DOROTHY HOLDEN

Charlottesville, Virginia; 1995; 60 × 40 inches; cotton; photograph by Erin Garvey

My QUILTS fall into five different categories: portrait, instructional, experimental, emotional, and inspirational. "Mr. and Mrs. Afro P. Angel and Michael" was purely inspirational. I don't know exactly when the idea hit me, but I'd been reading about angels for a couple of years. And then I began a collection of black angels. Just asking clerks if they had any black angels was interesting. One day it dawned on me: "Hey, why not make my own angel? And why not make a family of angels?" Lo and behold, all the imported African fabrics hopped off my shelves, and other fabrics that I had picked up serendipitously, and fell into place! Why

Mr. Angel has yellow trash-bag ties for hair, I do not know. Perhaps a true angel guided my selections. Mrs. Angel, or Tough Love Angel, has painted steel-wool hair with a heart-shaped face, mouth, eyes, and heart-shaped embroidered eyebrows.

Pueblo Pictographs ❯
IDA SCHENCK

Denver, Colorado; 1996; 77 × 43 inches; hand appliquéd, machine and hand quilted; photograph by John Bonath

"PUEBLO PICTOGRAPHS" evolved from a workshop on needle-turn appliqué given by Kathryn Kuhn and Timmie Stewart. I was inspired by the complex symbolism of the stylized animal figures and the opportunity to use combinations of brilliant colors.

The Quilters

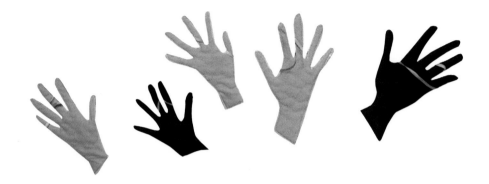

Cathleen R. Bailey
Pittsburgh, Pennsylvania

MY MATERNAL great-grandmother, Margaret Maynard, was a slave as a little girl. She could remember sitting on a fence when she was twelve, watching soldiers march through Fitzgerald, Georgia, proclaiming that all the slaves were free.

I learned sewing in home economics classes, but I was taught the fine art of sewing by my mother, Christine Shefton Richardson, and my sisters Dorothy Richardson Boyden and Evelyn Richardson Sherman. Garments could not be "hippity-hoppity" or "mammy-made," or else they would be a joke. I learned early on that you didn't want black women laughing at your creations.

For twenty years, I typed for various corporations. In September 1993, burdened with unfulfillment, I slipped a resignation letter onto my boss's desk. My good friend Eric Rucker and I co-founded Drums of West Africa in America. Eric taught me how to drum, and I made the costumes for the group. Then I had dreams about dolls and quilts, which I began to create.

I had no quilting experience, so I read books and watched TV quilt shows, where white women taught me never to use too much yellow, and that red could be overpowering. I felt constricted. Then, in a dream, my ex-slave great-grandmother Margaret appeared and admonished me. "Throw all the colors together," she said. "They'll go. Won't they?" All the colors *do* go together. Thank you, women in my family. I'm loosened. I'm a smiling quilter.

◄ WILD THING
VIRGINIA R. HARRIS

Albuquerque, New Mexico; 1993; 77 × 87 inches; cotton, machine quilting; collection of Susan Gore; photograph by Virginia R. Harris

I COLLECT AFRICAN PRINT fabrics to use in kaleidoscope patterns. When I saw this pattern, a new kaleidoscope emerged. I was delighted by the way the different pieces of fabric came together into one vibrant whole, creating an entirely new and different dance than would have been possible alone. Though the triangles in this pattern and those in Euro-American patterns are the same, the placement is different and creates a distinct feeling of natural, yet ordered, wildness.

Janet Waters Bailey
Baltimore, Maryland

I COME from a family that shared in bringing a multitude of fiber and sewing skills to my work. By age seven, I was designing clothes patterns, as well as hand sewing and knitting for myself and my dolls. I continued expanding my skills and creativity throughout high school and college, where I earned a B.A. in fine arts. In 1976 I hung up my artistic hat to pursue a sales and marketing career, working with health and beauty aid companies like Revlon and Gillette. But in 1991, with the encouragement of my jazz musician husband, Lester, I unboxed my old tools and began painting and weaving again on the weekends. My work has expanded and grown to what you see today.

ABOVE: *Detail from "Ties that Bind"*

E. Loretta Ballard

East Point, Georgia

WHEN I was the program director for a senior citizens center, I always admired the quilts the seniors made. But my own people did mostly crochet and knitting. I wasn't really introduced to quilting until the 1970s. Viola Canady came to the center to teach, and I took advantage of her courses. Long before learning to quilt, I had learned to batik. Now I combine my batik work with my quilts to create narratives about my childhood and family.

Quilting has given me an opportunity to keep the memory of my childhood alive. I come from a very large family and truly enjoyed every moment of my childhood. Most of the homes and buildings in the city that I grew up in are now gone. Making story quilts is my way of celebrating my memories of growing up. I don't ever want to forget my family and my hometown.

Sandy Barrett Hassan

Washington, D.C.

I LEARNED to sew in home economics classes during the 1950s. Following a North Carolina tradition, I began quilting in the early 1970s by making crib quilts for my daughters and baby shower gifts for friends and family members. I firmly believe that every newborn deserves a handmade quilt to cuddle up with.

I describe myself as a "fabric junkie." I have fabrics in my collection that I just look at in awe and hesitate to cut. I've been collecting fabric for over thirty years. Quilting is like therapy. I'm not a patient person, and quilting requires that I be still, quiet, and reflective. With needle and thread in hand, I'm centered and at peace with myself and the world.

It is the process rather than the end product that I enjoy most. The finished quilt is, for me, a reference point for the next project. There is a lesson to be learned from each piece. The lesson may have to do with color or technique. Or it may have to do with life—with forgiveness, passion, or justice.

Sandy Benjamin-Hannibal

Brooklyn, New York

QUILTS have completely caught my attention. I want to know how to make them, show them, print fabrics for them, conserve them, and so I am a fiber artist, teacher, researcher, lecturer, and quilt conservator. I have childhood memories of playing around and under the large frames at the quilting bees that my mother either hosted or participated in. Mama made quilts to warm the family, but none of those treasured heirlooms survived our use and her big, black laundry boiling pot! Years later, I watched and learned as she completed many beautiful coverings that were lovingly presented to children, grandchildren, friends, and charities.

I started quilting in the late 1970s, then flirted with the process for more than ten years. I didn't think of myself as a quilter, because I was creating quilted pot holders, table mats, and oven mitts, not quilts. When my mother lapsed into immobility due to an extended illness in 1989, I began to focus on quiltmaking. I wanted to show my mother what she had given me, and I wanted to create a gift she could use while she sat in her chair, recovering. I needed to participate in my mother's healing process, even from a distance. I knew my quilt would wrap her in the texture of my presence. Happily it worked, and I felt fulfilled and satisfied. From then on, quilting had me hooked!

Gerry Benton

Pittsburg, Pennsylvania

MY FIRST quilting exposure was at the African-American Heritage Quilt Show in August 1989. Every wall in the room held a celebration of color and folklore. These art quilts started my interest in the group and in quilting.

I am an artist with a passion for quilting. In fact, I retired from Bell Telephone in 1994 to pursue a career as a quilt instructor. My grandmother, Rose Salter, was also a quilter. She enjoyed using bright earthy colors. I must have inherited her sense of color.

ABOVE: *Detail from "Reprise"*

Hazel Rodney Blackman

Bronx, New York

My STUDIES in my native Jamaica, the United States, and Africa have inspired my use of vivid colors, and I use multimedia to give three-dimensional, lifelike vigor to my work. After I studied formally at the Traphagen School of Fashion in New York City, I went on to become one of the first American fashion designers of color. I was a designer for the National Cotton Council and for the Denim Council, and my work appeared in *Vogue, McCall's, Glamour*, and *Mademoiselle*. As owner and principal designer of Manhattan's African Tree House boutique, I specialized in adapting African fabrics and designs to the demands of everyday American life. Now my paintings and sculptured figures have been shown in galleries and museums in the United States, the Caribbean, Great Britain, and Europe.

Nedra Bonds

Kansas City, Kansas

I WAS taught to quilt by my grandmother at age six. At that time she told me that she needed to start on my hope chest. I now teach art appreciation and use my quilts as examples of universal symbolism. My quilts are inspired by my life experiences: I want them to make a statement concerning the social and political issues that touch the lives of people of color. I plan to pass the quilting tradition on to my own granddaughter.

Mary Bedford Brewer

Palmdale, California

IT SEEMS that I've sewn all my life. My mother, Ollie Mae King, has a wonderful memory of my learning to sew at age three or four, paper piecing with her quilt scraps. I always expected to sew like her, making clothing as well as quilts. After an eighth-grade sewing class in Kansas City, Kansas, I began to sew all types of clothing. My first quilt was a hand-appliquéd, machine-quilted crib quilt that I made for my daughter in 1956. Working with my hands centers me. It helps me get back to my source and reminds me of God's blessings.

While living in Colorado, I began a business repairing and finishing quilts. This soon expanded into creating computer fabric labels that provided the quilt's history and the quilter's photograph. My husband, James, is the graphic artist in our quilt documentation business. I've coordinated many friendship quilts and now have a wonderful collection; they are a happy reminder of how much I have gained in friendship, love, and support from quilting.

Tina Brewer

Pittsburgh, Pennsylvania

APPRECIATING our cultural past is extremely rewarding to me, and being able to interpret African American history through the art of quilting has been a blessing. When I quilt, there is a certain kind of spirituality and connectedness to the ancestors that balances and fuels me. Letting the cloth speak for these ancestors does much to define who I am and the direction in which I should go. Because my life is one of constant motion, I don't always know where these voices from the past are sending me. But I follow these ancient voices of wisdom, these voices of Africa.

Myrah Brown-Green

Brooklyn, New York

DURING my childhood in Cambridge, Massachusetts, I already knew that sewing and textiles would be a great part of my future. The women in my family did not quilt, but they had mastered the arts of crochet, knitting, and embroidery. My mother taught me how to sew when I was very young and gave me my first sewing machine when I graduated from high school. Years after graduating from the Pratt Institute, I was introduced to the wonderful world of quiltmaking by a very dear friend. From then on, I have experimented with a variety of quilt-making techniques and patterns.

Quiltmaking takes me through a wonderful, breathtaking "rite of passage." Because the experience is so beautiful, I continue to overflow with ideas, patterns, and colorful visions that can be shared with my family, friends, and the world.

Viola Burley-Leake
Washington, D.C.

I SEE my works as pieces of life's fabric sewn and stitched together, appliquéd, stuffed, sometimes painted, drawn, or fused to compose a story. First I look for a message or concept; then the fun begins. The joy is in not knowing exactly what the final work will look like. Although I start with sketches and patterns, the picture changes until it evolves into itself. Every layer, each success, and each mistake make the art. Like life, it is the journey to completion that makes it interesting.

Unlike traditional quilts made by putting together geometric patterns, my work is more pictorial, like appliquéd tapestries. I hope to share my excitement with others by showing them a perspective that is always changing, never boring.

Carolyn W. Cameron
Kansas City, Kansas

FABRIC speaks to me of the lives, customs, and traditions of many peoples and many cultures, past and present. I am influenced in much of my work by the way fabric is an inter- and intracultural strand, weaving all of our lives together. Merging commonly accepted fabric (cloth) with uncommonly accepted fabric (paper), creating unusual shapes and textures, and playing with the intrigue of light upon fabric surfaces and silken threads, are all especially important to me. I think my work reflects the sensuality of light and rhythm upon fabric and design.

Cynthia H. Catlin
Aurora, Colorado

QUILTING caught my interest at the age of thirteen, when I started sewing clothes. I saved all the scraps and began hand-piecing them into quilt tops under the guidance of my maternal grandparents. I credit my grandmother with helping me develop accurate piecing methods, and my grandfather with giving me a wonderful sense of color. My grandparents were prolific quilters, and as far back as I can remember a quilt was always in some stage of creative development at their house. Quilting now gives me the joy of continuing the legacy of my maternal grandparents and my husband's grandmother. Following in the spiritual and creative footsteps of my ancestors, I design my pieces using contemporary fabrics and methods. My designs include custom-made quilts, wearable art, and wall hangings for public and private interior spaces.

Chris Clark
Birmingham, Alabama

AS A BOY growing up in Birmingham, Alabama, I never figured I would end up as an artist. It wasn't until years later, after attending Livingston University and doing a stint in the army, that I began to think about art as something I could do. While recuperating from an illness, I began to paint pictures, usually on slabs of wood I found at flea markets. In 1989 I asked my grandmother to show me how to quilt. She taught me the basic stitches, passed down from her grandmother, and soon I had stitched together my own quilt. My next instinct was to paint directly onto the quilt. I hadn't set out to do that, but the picture I painted was just beautiful, so I did another one, and so on.

Soon I made friends in the art world. Today my quilts and furniture are featured in many exhibits, museums, and galleries. I was a featured artist in the book *Revelation, Alabama's Visionary Folk Artists*, and my work is in the permanent collection at the Birmingham Museum of Art.

Della Collins
Houston, Texas

I HAVE always admired quilts, but over the years I was primarily involved in making clothing—out of necessity—for my very petite daughters. I collected the fabric for their clothes from remnants of my own clothing and those of other dressmakers. Then one day the phrase "wearable art" became fashionable and I was in the limelight. I put on one of the very first exhibitions of art wearables. I kept hearing, however, that African Americans "couldn't do" and "didn't do" certain kinds of quilts, and I got tired of it. Never intending to make quilts, I asked Karey Bresenhan, founder of the Houston International Quilt Exhibition, if I could curate an exhibition of African American quilts. I wanted to show that all African Americans did not make quilts with crooked seams, big stitches, and patterns that were not sewn together properly. I wanted to dispel the myth that we couldn't produce well-made traditional and art quilts. The Guild members insisted that I have a quilt of my own in the exhibition, and this is how I came to make my very first quilt. Most of the quilts that I now make are small wall hangings, but I've decided to make larger quilts as my time permits.

Donnette A. Cooper
Hyattsville, Maryland

I WAS born and raised in Kingston, Jamaica, and moved to the United States in 1975 to attend college. I am a graduate of Clark University, Howard University School of Law, and the Norman Manley School of Law at the University of the West Indies, in Jamaica. I currently practice law in Washington, D.C.

Without any formal art training, I began quilting in 1991 after experimenting with clothing, furniture, and jewelry design. Among my influences are my father, Daniel George Cooper, a tailor of exceptional ability and dedication to his art; my grandmother, May Lyons, who introduced me to sewing; a number of Jamaican artists, including batik artist Dawn Scott, potter Norma Harrack, and silk-screener Beti Campbell; my exploration of African art, particularly textile design; and finally the rich, resilient, and varied texture of the Jamaican cultural landscape. My quilts combine African textiles, self-dyed fabrics, and African and Caribbean design elements to capture an African Diaspora aesthetic.

Adriene Cruz
Portland, Oregon

I WAS born in Harlem, New York. Greatly influenced by my mother's passion for color, I attended the High School of Art and Design and received a B.F.A. from the School of Visual Arts in New York. I've been an artist for as long as I can remember, and try my best to share my gift so others can awaken their artist within. I'm moved by a passion for color, a love of symbols, and a deep interest in matters of the spirit. Blending these elements allows me to keep the rhythm of my roots alive.

My art fulfills a powerful desire to express visually what cannot be spoken. These quilts are meditation quilts because of the spiritual journey I experience during each creation. I was not always conscious of ancestral connection and creativity. For me, the power of art beyond its visual image is developed over time—the power born of the spirit, of roots, and of the celebration of survival.

OPPOSITE: *Detail from "Pueblo Pictographs"*
LEFT: *Detail from "Guess Who's Coming to Dinner"*

Michael Cummings

New York, New York

I DRAW inspiration from ancient cultures and modern art, from Africa and the art of African Americans. I am concerned as much with art as with craft. The narrative themes in my quilts are constructed sometimes with dense designs, making statements that can be humorous or somber. The juxtaposition of contrasting colors dominates my creative thought process, both in technique and in design development.

Francelise Dawkins

Glens Falls, New York

AFTER a decade of exploring paper collages, my adventures with textile collages started in the 1980s with the idea of creating a meditative concept for interior designs. I first coined the term "silkollage" in 1988, then "ethnikollage" in 1992, to reflect both my multirooted background and the fact that Asian silks as well as African and European printed fabrics had started to appear in my work.

Being of Caribbean Indian, African, and European descent, multilingual and a self-rescued derailed lefty, I have always been intimately aware of the diversity of the world. I use the  fluid, shapable medium of textile to express my awareness that individuality is the authentic path to unity.

In the way polyphony works in African music, my hyphenated heritage achieves balance from the combinations of techniques, colors, and shapes in my work. I now create sculptural pieces that are inspired by the bold luminosity of my Caribbean mother's work. They can be "Africanized" with mystery and warmth, and even "pastellized," reflecting upstate New York's sunless moods, depending on what cultural wavelength I am on when creating. To make my experience visible and simply let it flow is what counts.

L'Merchie Frazier

Roxbury, Massachusetts

LIFE IS an exploration of life, death, and rebirth, and I celebrate this journey through my work, which I've called "Save Me From My Amnesia." The recovery of memory fragments—from our beginnings in the Garden (Nubia), through our Middle Passage and our rebirth here in the Americas—provides the basis for my art, whether it is visual, in performance, or written. The shedding of amnesia develops from the slow recall of our connections to the Motherland, connections that survived slavery and colonialism. Whether I'm working with quilts, beads, silk batik, or metals, these images serve as threads of memory that trigger recognition, salvation, redemption.

I find that textile designs emit a presence, a spirit, an energy, a vitality unlike that of any other medium. My use of beads and textile designs stems from a heritage passed on from my maternal grandfather, a tailor and embroiderer, to my mother, an excellent craftswoman in textiles and beadwork, and finally to me. Quilting provides me with an inexhaustible documentation of our cultural voice. Quilting rejoins the fragments and reconnects the members. Quilting re-members.

Roland L. Freeman

Washington, D.C.

ROLAND FREEMAN is an internationally recognized photodocumentarian whose work has been exhibited worldwide. He has been a field research photographer for the Smithsonian Institution for more than twenty years and has been recognized through awards and grants from the National Endowment for the Arts, the National Endowment for the Humanities, and the National Black Arts Festival through its 1994 Living Legend Award. Among the first to call attention to the quilts made by African Americans, he authored the groundbreaking book *Something to Keep You Warm*, and was curator for the accompanying exhibition. He is an avid collector of African American quilts, and a quilt designer as well. Roland Freeman is a beloved figure in the African American quilting community. He is also the author of the book *A Communion of the Spirits: African American Quilters, Preservers, and Their Stories.*

Sandra K. German
Loveland, Ohio

I GREW UP without roots, and at times was homeless as a child. The echoes of my childhood haunt me still. Art came to me early in life, but I did not acknowledge or honor it until just recently. Now I see that art has taught me to know myself. It has tilled the soil of my soul and helped me, at long last, to put down roots. It has helped me *own* my self.

When I was eighteen, I was told that I would be blind within ten years. I then embarked upon an orgy of "active" seeing, embracing objects and images as though I had to see enough to last a lifetime. Some thirty years later, my vision is still adequate, but my commitment to active seeing is as strong as ever.

As I work, I am consciously aware of the ancestral tradition, the "laying on of hands." I feel this is why so many people regard quilts as objects that can both warm the body and touch the heart. I know that hope can heal, and it is my ever-present "hands-on" prayer that those who view my work will carry away with them a renewed sense of hope.

Frances Hare
Rochester, New York

W HEN I was around the age of nine, my mother enrolled me in summer camp, where we were always working on some craft project or other. It was there that I first discovered a talent for quilting. In 1974 I graduated from the State University College at Buffalo with a B.A. in liberal arts. It was there that my passion and talent evolved into a skill that became a source of much joy and labor, only to be interrupted, then united, with my second passion, dance.

From 1981 to 1987 I danced professionally with Garth Fagan Dance. Working with Mr. Fagan and the company heightened my self-confidence and enabled me to pursue my commitment to working as a fabric artist. My work now is about the movement inherent in everyday objects, the polyrhythms of texture, and the nuance and depth of color. My intent is to offer the viewer a host of ideas on how he or she might want to interact with the work, be it functional or artistic.

Carole Harris
Detroit, Michigan

I T IS NO coincidence that the titles of many of works refer to music and movement. Motion, rhythm, and harmony are terms used when discussing music, poetry, painting, and dance, but I find these terms are also appropriate to the process and definition of my work. The creative process has led me to discover cultural connections I was not aware of thirty years ago, when I made my first quilt.

Beginning with that first quilt, and proceeding with the caution and precision dictated by a formal Western aesthetic, I continued to learn the craft of piecing. But I became bored and dissatisfied with what was, to me, the sameness and predictability of traditional quilt patterns. I began to explore various ways of manipulating fabric within the quilt-making context. This improvisation liberated me, as it has other artists in music, dance, literature, and the visual arts, and it allowed me to revel in the process of discovery. Improvisation continues to lead me on an uncharted journey, a journey that has taken me back to the be-bop, boogie-woogie, and blues of northern migrants; to the work songs and field hollers of the enslaved; to the Egungun and Gelede celebrations of my African ancestors; and back again to Duke Ellington, Don Pullen, rap, and hip-hop.

ABOVE: *Detail from "African Skies and Southern Soil"*

Virginia R. Harris
Albuquerque, New Mexico

FOR YEARS I searched for a creative outlet that would engender in me the passion of which other artists speak. In 1991 a friend asked me to make a quilt square for her fiftieth birthday. I checked out six books from the library and made a block. I then made a second block because I didn't like the first one. The next day I bought fabric to make a quilt. I felt as if I had come home; the experience changed my relationship to the world.

Through quilting, I have learned to embrace my own personal aesthetic. Piecing together varied colors, shapes, and fabrics brings to light the variety and diversity of who I am. My quilts are inspired by many sources; they are based on traditional African and Japanese designs, on origami, nature, life challenges, and my own vision. The jobs I have held and the education I acquired served as the foundation on which my life was built. Much of that foundation had to be dismantled and rebuilt to fit the person I have become. I will continue to seek my truths, to live a life of honesty and integrity, with compassion for myself and for others.

Peggie L. Hartwell
New York, New York

WHEN I was growing up on our farm in South Carolina, I had the good fortune to live in a household of extended family members, where some of the men were great storytellers. Among them, however, was one master storyteller whose voice penetrated all of our senses as though laced with honey. This was my grandfather, William Tyler, Sr. His stories were so passionate—so alive—he all but sang them like living epics. As I sat at his feet soaking up his every word, I had no idea that he was leaving me a legacy of storytelling. The only difference between us is that my grandfather told his stories in the oral tradition and I now tell mine through pictorial quilts. Narrative quiltmaking has become my voice on cloth. It has allowed me to go back in time and to recapture my childhood and a tradition of farm life that no longer exists. Because a great deal of my work is autobiographical, it allows me to continue in the tradition of my grandfather.

Kyra E. Hicks
Kansas City, Missouri

TWO experiences led me to create my own quilts. The first took place several years ago at the Afro-American Museum in Los Angeles, when I saw a quilt by Michael Cummings that depicted his grandmother on her front porch. I could almost hear his grandmother call out a greeting to her neighbors. This was the first time that fabrics "spoke" to me. The second experience was in 1991, at an exhibit on African American story quilts since slavery, at the Taft Museum in Cincinnati, Ohio. While walking among the quilts, I knew that I also wanted to tell stories with fabrics, although the only previous sewing experience I had had was in seventh grade. To date, I have still not had any formal quilting training or classes.

My quilts are generally inspired by personal experiences and daily observations. I combine written words with pictures to make specific statements. I want the quilts to be pleasing to the eye as well as thought-provoking. Someone told me once that viewing my quilts was like reading a person's diary.

Dorothy Holden
Charlottesville, Virginia

I CREATE quilts that are unique in materials as well as subject matter. You can find everything in my works from bag ties and steel wool, to socks and neckties, to weeds and vines. Most of my commissions have been for portraits and traditional quilts, in which I try to express a warm, casual, and frequently humorous attitude.

Patricia Johnson

Hampton, Virginia

MY FIRST exposure to quilting was at a workshop taught by a very talented fiber artist named Lethia Robertson. I later saw an exhibit of her work and was amazed at her creative use of color and fabrics. Although I made many of my own clothes, I did not think that I had the talent for quilting.

Several years later, I moved to Hampton, Virginia, and soon joined the Golden Thimble Needlecraft Guild, which sparked my interest in quilting again, along with other types of needlework. I also attended workshops at quilt shows and local quilt shops. I then joined the 54-40 African-American Quilters Guild. This guild came out of a workshop taught by Loretta Craig and was named after a quilt pattern she uses exclusively in her work.

Helen A. Kearney-Thobhani

Littleton, Colorado

I BECAME involved in quilting when my uncle asked me to repair a quilt made by his paternal grandmother, Susan Anna Kearney. I am a materials chemist who sees quilting as an extension of chemistry, because quilting is also an activity where I can exercise my creative intelligence.

Sharon Kerry-Harlan

Wauwatosa, Wisconsin

I NEVER cease to be amazed at what our society discards. We don't realize how many new ideas and inspired possibilities we lose when we cast aside unwanted materials. I have rescued many a bauble, bead, and button from the trash and sewn them into my fabric collage quilt tops. Once these salvaged artifacts are needled on, they become transformed and take on new meaning within the context of the whole piece. To me, my quilts preserve "rescued memories" that serve as cultural symbols and personal records for future generations.

Over the past four years, an obsession with the treasure scenes in classic high-seas movies has led me to embellish my quilt tops with the recycled bounty of rescued objects. When collecting artifacts for my quilts, I always feel as if I'm in search of "hidden treasure." I constantly hunt for and experiment with different types of cloth, threads, and three-dimensional objects to add texture and depth to my quilts. And when all the elements come together, I hope viewers feel surprised and ultimately elated by their discoveries of this once-forgotten memorabilia.

Betty Leacraft

Philadelphia, Pennsylvania

I WAS ENCOURAGED to sew at the age of five by my maternal grandmother, whose own mother had been a professional seamstress in North Carolina during the 1800s. My paternal grandmother also made quilts, clothing, and needle lace, and taught all of her female children the art of quiltmaking. Ironically my mother does not sew, but I feel a responsibility to rekindle the creative flame that burned in the generation before me. This inspires me to teach this craft to others and to share these valuable life skills.

As a child, my interest in world cultures was fostered by my grandfather, a native of Georgetown, Guyana. The creation of my own clothing, my apprenticeships with local ethnic designers, and my fascination with the textiles, garments, and adornments of African and other cultures led to further cultural education. I also entered a process of self-directed research, a highlight of which was my cultural studies in Bahia, Brazil.

The format of my work ranges from textile constructions, which often include mixed-media floor installations, to wearable art and soft sculpture. I use machine and hand sewing, combined with surface design, embellishment, found objects, and nontraditional materials. I like to create works that blur the lines between quilts, wall hangings, wearable art, sculpture, and installation. The symbolism, inspiration, and design of my work is based on the textiles, garments, rituals, ceremonial objects, and adornments of the African Diaspora.

OPPOSITE: *Detail from "Star Line"*

Charlotte Lewis
Portland, Oregon

MY GRANDMOTHER was a quilt advocate and artist, and in the past I made quilts for family and friends, but it wasn't until five years ago that I recognized the importance of her stitching in my life. I am a graduate of the Portland Museum Art School and worked for many years as an artist of multimedia paintings, graphics, and sculpture. My new appreciation focused upon a connection to African traditions. Drawing from these links to our ancestral paths, I now work mostly with cotton fiber, stamping and stenciling designs of symbols and icons, threading and stitching beads and sequins. Through this work, I hope to communicate, educate, and reach out to others.

Carole Y. Lyles
Columbia, Maryland

I AM A largely self-taught artist and a woman of color. Art has always been part of my life, and I experimented with many types of media before textile art found me. In the summer of 1990, I decided to begin quiltmaking without knowing anything about it at all. I later discovered that a great-great-ancestor of mine had been an accomplished quilter. Sometimes I believe that her spirit called me to this work.

The books I read about quilts taught me the history of traditional European American quiltmaking, but I did not find it an entirely suitable vocabulary with which to express my own visions. Later, I learned about the textile art of Africa and Asia, and now I fuse and transform all three traditions in my work. My quilts reflect a number of visual influences: Postimpressionist painting, the sacred object tradition of the *minkis*, the Bauhaus school, paintings by Lois Mailou Jones and Romare Bearden, Ethiopian liturgical art, Kandinsky and Klee, and so much more.

Some people ask me why I create this work, and why I have chosen this medium. The answer is that I love fiber, its weight, its color, the smell of natural dyes in the cotton, the cool swish of silk. I feel gloriously blessed to be a textile artist.

Gwendolyn A. Magee
Jackson, Mississippi

SINCE early childhood, I have been fascinated by, and completely in love with, color, especially color that is intense and vibrant. However, it was not until I started quilting that I found a medium through which I could manipulate color to achieve the patterns and effects that please and excite me.

Throughout childhood, I was continually exposed to the arts by my mother, Annie Lee Jones. However, crafts were her passion, and many of my fondest memories are of the hours we spent together working on every type of craft imaginable, with the exception of quilting. Due to her influence, I have sustained a lifelong interest in the arts and in crafts.

I learned how to quilt out of a desire to create something tangible that my daughters, Kamili and Aliya, could take with them to college as an expression of my love and as a reminder of their home. Initially that was my sole objective; I never anticipated that quilting would so quickly become my primary outlet for creative expression.

My husband, D.E. Magee, Jr., and my daughters continue to be my greatest fans and most ardent supporters. Their admiration of and deep appreciation for the work I produce is the source of my inspiration.

Julianne McAdoo
Pittsburgh, Pennsylvania

MY INTEREST in quiltmaking originated from collecting antique quilts. I have always been drawn to old textiles. As a child, I was told that my great-grandmother, Emma Jackson, was a quiltmaker. Unfortunately, the many quilts she made did not survive to be passed on to my generation. In 1985, on a visit to the Carnegie Library, I happened upon a contemporary quilt exhibit. I was mesmerized by the exhibit, particularly the pictorial quilts. I immediately started taking quiltmaking classes. I am one of the founding members of the African American Heritage Quilters Guild in Pittsburgh.

I often tell people that quiltmaking helps me stay centered. As a corporate professional, I find the stresses associated with the workplace sometimes overwhelming. Quilting is the place I go to recharge my creative juices, to exercise my artistic muse and find my "center."

Dindga McCannon

New York, New York

I'VE BEEN a multimedia artist for the past thirty-four years, and have been making quilts since the late 1970s. Fabrics and a sewing machine have been in my life since I was a child. Both my mother and my grandmother sewed, crocheted, and did other kinds of needlework, which they passed down to me. I've always made "untraditional" quilts, in that they were meant for the wall instead of the bed. Creating wall quilts gives me the freedom to use a variety of materials, and I'm able to use all my fine arts training. I utilize painting on fabric, silk-screening, tie-dyeing, embroidery, beadwork, and sewing in my quilts. I can be a storyteller, an illustrator, or a collage artist via appliqué. There's always something about life to comment on through quiltmaking.

Winnie Akissi McQueen

Macon, Georgia

MY ADVENTURE here, as with all my artistic endeavors, is in experimenting with color; with dyeing and stamping surfaces and sometimes discharging dyes; and, more recently, in layering other objects onto surfaces to create additional dimensions. I have used my skills to explore ideas with universal appeal, employing symbols and images from both my African and American cultures. Today I am the storyteller working with Old World methods that are modified by New World technology.

OPPOSITE: *Detail from "All Life Begins in Darkness"*
ABOVE: *Detail from "Glow from the Motherland"*

Edjohnetta Miller

Hartford, Connecticut

I AM influenced by the colors and patterns of the natural world, the power and beauty of traditional African textiles, and the spirit of improvisation and play found at the heart of African American creativity. But more than anything else, it is my love of fabrics that attracts me to quilting. I want to create works that are visually challenging and pleasing. Textiles provide all the ways in which I enjoy expressing myself. I have form, color, balance, and harmony, all of which merge into satisfying creations.

I have designed a limited edition of cross-cultural quilts that are composed of textiles from a variety of countries and cultures. The cloth conveys my sense of how the cultures of the world can be woven into patterns that are both harmonious and unsettling. My improvisationally arranged, recycled fabrics express my sense of motion and color, and I delight in these new and unexpected combinations.

Jacquelyn Hughes Mooney

San Diego, California

THERE have been times in my life when I have been challenged to manage some rather monumental circumstances. My own survival demanded a heightened sensitivity to the nuances of human emotions. My art thus takes form through the process of opening my heart to the varied, and often subtle, sensibilities of the human experience.

Aline V. Moyler

Mt. Vernon, New York

AFTER many years of needlepointing; home sewing; painting; single-handedly bricking my entire backyard; becoming a weaver; having two daughters graduate from college; and finally having lost my advertising agency job to a merger; I discovered quilting! Over the past eight years, I have made many traditional quilts, but I eventually tired of duplicating designs thought out by someone else. My creative juices kicked in when I discovered that with the appliqué technique, I could express any idea or event on fabric.

Marlene O'Bryant-Seabrook
Charleston, South Carolina

I BEGAN quilting in 1982, when I observed a raffle quilt hanging in a high school. Shortly thereafter, I enrolled in an eight-week quilting course. The classes were held in an antique shop. On the first night, quilts that were more than one hundred years old were displayed. Because I had planned to make only one quilt, I was intrigued with the idea that my quilt could be around long after I was gone; I still feel a calming sense of being connected to the future while I am quilting.

I came to view myself as a quilter after meeting master quilter Marie Wilson in 1991. She endorsed my work and told me about the Women of Color Quilters Network. As a professional educator with a creative streak, I approach quilting with the dual perspective of educator and artist: O'Bryant-Seabrook the artist combines various techniques, such as appliqué, cross-stitch, photo transfer, and piecing; O'Bryant-Seabrook the educator slips a lesson into each quilt, such as love of God, family, and children; pride in heritage; or respect for accomplishments.

Doris Parker
Los Angeles, California

I WAS born in New Orleans, Louisiana. As a child I gathered scraps from my mother and aunt to make doll clothes for my Coke-bottle and clothespin dolls. No one in my family quilted; they made garments.

I moved to Los Angeles in 1944 and for twenty years worked in an embroidery shop, originally to earn money for my family to come out to L.A. After that, I took an art class for three years at South West College.

I was introduced to quilting at the African Market Place by the African American Quilters of Los Angeles. They had set up a booth of quilts to give to babies with life-threatening diseases. I made two blocks there; then I asked to take several blocks home and return them, completed, by mail. They asked me to join the guild in 1991. I have taken several classes and am still doing so. I am inspired by the beautiful work I see in quilt shows. I completed six quilts in 1996 (one for each of my children), and had several quilts on display at the A.A.Q.L.A. show in November that year.

Julia A. Payne
Denver, Colorado

I AM A self-taught quiltmaker and acquired the love of sewing from my mother, but I am what one would call a late bloomer. Although creativity has always been a part of my life, my entry into the field of art did not come about until after I had raised a family and decided that I had to find something to keep myself occupied. During my youth, however, it was considered quite unfeasible and outrageous to even consider such an occupation as a hobby, let alone a career.

Quilting is my favorite artistic endeavor. I see no difference between quilting and so-called fine art. To me they are one and the same, and this is how I approach my work.

Zene Peer
Milwaukee, Wisconsin

I AM A self-taught fiber artist. I have been working professionally at my craft since October 1992. I love designs that are bold, vibrant, and overflowing with the emotions and colors of my African-Jamaican-American heritage. I relate my use of color to filling in the pictures of a coloring book. I also use intricate hand embroidery, found objects, and African fabrics to create quilts that are unlike any in Grandma's closet.

My art is a gift from God, and it's personal! When I create a piece it is directed by spirits that surround and protect me. My quilts are inspired by experiences and feelings which, if you look closely, are no different from those of anyone else who connects to them.

ABOVE: *Detail from "Spirit in the Night"*

Edna J. Petty
East St. Louis, Illinois

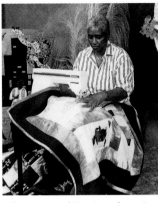

EVER SINCE I was a child, I knew that I wanted to create. Although I did not understand the concept of being an artist, I saw shapes in clouds, broken glass, and so on, and I began to draw the images I saw. Creating brought me the most joy in my young life.

My mother, Alberta Willis, quilted bedcovers, and I enjoyed cutting the fabric scraps for her. I took sewing throughout my high school years, and made money sewing for others as well as for myself. This continued into my married life, as I made special outfits for my husband and four children. The appliqué technique that I use in my art quilts came from the tragedy of losing my oldest son while I was still in graduate school. Putting my life back together was like piecing together a complicated puzzle, and that is now symbolic of my work.

While in college, I discovered the African American artists Barbara Chase-Riboud and Faith Ringgold, and felt a great joy in being able to call myself an artist and live my dream. My inspiration comes from my environment, people, music, and life in general. I use an appliqué/collage technique to create the quilts. In the beginning I did all of my stitching by hand, but that was too slow for me, so I began to construct my quilts by machine. I love an abundance of color, designs, and patterns, and on occasion incorporate found objects in a piece, to see how or if they work together. And more than anything, I pray, and meditate, and write down my thoughts, and the creative process develops.

Barbara Pietila
Baltimore, Maryland

I DRAW inspiration for my work from everyday life and from my childhood, which was rich with conversations, many relatives, and special occasions. I believe that all quilts tell a story, either in the history of the fabrics, in the pattern, or in the making of the quilt. I try to carry on that same tradition by creating scenes that give the viewer some idea of what my life is like.

Michaeline Reed
Pittsburgh, Pennsylvania

ONE FATEFUL day in 1981, while waiting in the car for my husband to come out of the bank, I looked up at a building across the street and saw a sign that read "City Quilt Shop." Little did I know then what a profound effect it would have on my life. I had sewn clothing since I was nine, so I was no stranger to fabric stores, but when I went into that shop, it was as if I'd entered a new world. I was hooked from my first quiltmaking lesson.

I draw inspiration for my quilts from my surroundings: nature, people, music, family events, and stories. I am always trying to improve my work, and have taken classes from many prominent fiber artists. I teach quilting and various embellishment techniques because I feel that it is important to pass this beautiful art form on to those who will follow us.

Kenneth H. Roper
Castle Rock, Colorado

FOR ME, making a quilt serves two purposes. First, it provides a great escape from the everyday work and grind of being a CPA. The second, which is much more valuable to me, is that it gives me the chance to remember Hessie and think of the "good old days." Hessie was my grandmother, and the "good old days" were when I, as a young child, would sit and watch her piece quilting by hand. I remember the wooden quilting horses she used and how they would take up a whole room. Hessie's father was a black Methodist minister and her mother was Native American. Quilting for them meant producing something functional, especially in the winter months. Hessie began quilting when she was only eight. She made a Double Wedding Ring quilt for my wife and me when we got married. Needless to say, it is one of our most cherished possessions.

I started quilting in 1984, after visiting Hessie on a trip home to Oklahoma. She and I were discussing her inability to quilt anymore. She was ninety-eight at the time. She "dared" me to try it, and by the next summer I'd made my first quilt. I even designed it. Since then I've made twenty-four, all by machine. Every time I start a project I think of my grandmother and remember how she would use old newsletters to make her templates. When I finish it, I ask my wife and daughters the rhetorical question "Wonder what Hessie would say?"

Ida Schenck

Denver, Colorado

AFTER receiving a Ph.D. in music history from Northwestern University, I had a wonderful career as a professor of music history at Metropolitan State College in Denver. Now that I have retired, I have had time to learn to quilt and begin a new career. I have been involved in the needle arts since the age of eleven or twelve, when my aunt taught me to crochet and I learned to sew in a home economics class. Since then, I have been involved with sewing, crocheting, knitting, cross-stitch, and needlepoint. As a small child, I remember seeing my grandmother and her friends meet and quilt, but I did not get involved in the art of quilting until two years ago. I am now hooked. Through workshops, videos, how-to books, and magazines, I'm learning as many techniques as possible. I have gravitated toward thematic quilts and am most inspired by the iconography and history of early cultures: African, American Indian, and pre-Columbian.

Elizabeth Scott

Baltimore, Maryland

I COME from a long line of quilters, weavers, and sharecroppers. From plow to quilt I know about. Eleven of us lived together; I was one of seven girls. We worked year-round, sun-up to sundown, with no time for play. "Busy hands, busy minds" was what my mother told us when we complained about the work. I remember a time when my family collected flawed material from factory refuse bins. Sometimes muslin patches could be bought for 10 cents a bunch. Sometimes the same amount bought yards of material—a stained tablecloth or pieces of bolts where the dye had bled. Our father would redye the scraps with black, red, or yellow pigment from clay he'd gathered and heated. Our mother made clothes and bedclothes from material not used for quilts.

Joyce Scott

Baltimore, Maryland

PAINTING is a harsh medium. Traditionally it's been male-dominated, and many of the most famous painters either went crazy or weren't recognized until after their deaths. Fabrics, on the other hand, are accessible. There are no set rules. It's all common sense. Painting is exclusive, but arts like quilting are inclusive.

Sandra Smith

Silver Spring, Maryland

WHEN I'm not at work, I can be found designing quilts and wall hangings. I've been interested in sewing since childhood. My interest began in the 1960s, when my parents encouraged me to pursue sewing by getting me patterns, fabric, and a sewing machine. They encouraged me to make clothes for my dolls. I graduated from Barbie to making clothes for myself. When I was in college, I made clothes for people to raise money for tuition. Ten years later I began quilting. Initially my quilts were purely utilitarian, but my current works are decorative art pieces made specifically for the wall.

I enjoy working with intricate quilt patterns and a multitude of colors. I tend to use bright reds and oranges. Most of my quilts are asymmetrical, with nonrepetitive block patterns. I also enjoy searching for fabric. My hobby has become a passion, and sometimes I wish that my regular job didn't get in the way!

Jim Smoote

Chicago, Illinois

AT A VERY early age I discovered an aptitude for drawing, an ability that was recognized and supported by my parents and instructors. At the School of the Art Institute of Chicago, I studied under two weavers, both of whom had studied at the Bauhaus. I developed an interest in African and folk textiles, as well as printed fabrics from the 1920s and '30s. I eventually gravitated toward the surface decoration of fabrics, because it offered me more flexibility as an artist. I have been exploring mask and fetish images for almost twenty years, primarily through endless applications of fiber and fabric. Now, however, my work explores humor, contemporary urban (hip-hop) images, the political, or the provocative. I create primarily quilted pieces with acrylic paint and various other traditional and nontraditional techniques and materials. My work has provided me with great enjoyment, and has afforded me the opportunity to travel and exhibit not only here in the United States, but also in Africa, South America, and Europe.

Ana Arzu Titus
New York, New York

IN OUR many roles as friends and lovers, mothers and sisters, we laugh, cry, contemplate, support, suffer, and struggle. Through all this, we continually develop and grow. All of my pictorial quilts are freeze frames that capture the moments when this evolutionary process actually occurs. The prevalent theme in all my quilts is women discovering the dignity in their lives as they undergo the experiences of seeking, loving, losing, and winning. In many ways, my quilts reflect my own spiritual path and evolution as a woman. My style is a collaborative work between my creative energy and the inherent will of the fabric. The results are pieces that emit life beyond the ability of fabric to do so alone.

Vivian M. Walker
Hampton, Virginia

I HAVE sewn for most of my life. My grandmother took in laundry, and she always sat down to iron. The ironing board sat right beside the dining room table in our old farmhouse. Some of my earliest memories are of her sitting at the ironing board, telling me how to cut the scraps of fabric my mother discarded, sew them, and fashion beautiful doll clothes for all of my dolls. Later I took sewing classes in junior high school, high school, and college. I found the creative process to be very therapeutic. Sewing was where I went when the world got to be too much.

I came to quilting about five years ago. I was fascinated with the way the blocks, the patterns, the texture, and the tones all came together; and the way colors and shapes played off one another. I became obsessed with quilting in a way that I would have never dreamed possible. When I'm quilting, I am transported to a place of peace and serenity.

I have not sold or exhibited any of my work. Right now, I feel something much deeper when I quilt—that I am creating heirlooms for those who will follow. I want my quilts to be there for children not yet born, to wrap them in, and for someone to tell these children the story of me, or my quilt, or both. Like my quilts, I am a work in progress, and am constantly growing and becoming better. While I am on this journey, I will follow my quilts wherever they take me, and delight in every step along the way.

Brenetta Ward
Seattle, Washington

MY PASSION for quilting began when I was a young girl, watching my aunt Alma and her friends making beautiful quilts for church bazaars. Each summer I was sent to Royal Lakes, Illinois, to stay with Aunt Alma, and each summer she would teach me the art of quilting. We would spend hours piecing brightly colored tops and then hand-quilting the layers together. Only years later did I realize that her quilt patterns reflected the legacy of our Mississippi and African ancestors.

Cloth with vivid colors and flowing designs inspires me. The joy of quilting comes from selecting just the right fabrics, then moving shapes around into patterns until they click. Combining my traditional patchwork skills and my hand-quilting techniques with my love of African textiles enables me to create unusual designs. Quilting lets me express ideas that are uniquely mine.

Ruth A. Ward
Pittsburgh, Pennsylvania

MY GRANDMOTHER quilted because she needed to make covers for the bed. I remember playing under her large quilting frame, which hung from the ceiling. I am not sure if it was the memory that led me to the art of quilting, or if it was all the clothes that I made for myself and my family, or if it was the colors and the feel of the fabrics. In 1988, while I was recovering from a bout of multiple sclerosis, a friend and I would visit each week to quilt and share designs and quilting techniques. Soon after, I joined the African American Heritage Quilters Guild, and I've been quilting ever since.

Yvonne Wells
Tuscaloosa, Alabama

QUILTING is something that I observed my mother do but did not participate in. I started quilting in 1979 out of a need to express myself. Initially, I made traditional quilt patterns, but I was continually drawn to "doing my own thing" with those patterns. In 1985 I was persuaded to show my work at the Kentucky Festival, an arts and crafts event that features about 80 to 100 arts and crafts people and attracts 60,000 visitors. I was awarded "Best of Show."

Since that time, I have received many accolades. I even contributed a square for the White House Christmas tree skirt and a stuffed heart for the tree. The square represented the state of Alabama.

Sherry Whetstone-McCall
Kansas City, Missouri

I'M OBSESSED, I admit it. It seems that fabrics have fascinated me ever since conception. There is a mysterious aura about fabric that lures me in for a closer look and a gentle caress. It awakens an uncontrollable urge to create images that will make me, the viewer, stand in awe. That fascination eventually turned into a B.S. degree in clothing, textiles, and merchandising. Now, at thirty-something, I am turning my obsession into a three-dimensional art form.

My choices of textiles are as diverse as my images; I'll use everything from cotton to silk brocades to capture my thoughts. When I look at a piece of fabric, exciting textures and intricate patterns transform into a wonderful work of art right before my eyes. It's like magic. I love to experiment with various sewing techniques, choosing the ones that will bring out the true personality of the cloth.

As a textile artist, I want my images to exude a magnetic quality that will draw the viewer in for intimate inspection. I want the viewers to seek and find all the little "Sherry things" that are hidden in each piece. Creating the element of surprise and delight in my work is just a natural part of the process. The little kid in me sometimes shows up in my work; it's really fun letting my hands tell my mind what to do for a change.

Deborah Willis
Washington, D.C.

MY FAMILY has always quilted. My maternal grandmother had thirteen children and recycled clothing, blankets, and other hand-me-downs until they were no longer recognizable in their original form. She would then make quilts of the salvageable items. She gave quilts to her children throughout her eighty-eight years. My paternal great-aunt, Cora, was also a quilter, ceramist, and canner. Visiting her as a child in the early 1950s, I marveled at the fact that she called herself an artist. My work is influenced by these two women as well as artists and friends.

My work is based on social concerns that touch the African American family as well as political issues that address the oppressed. I reinterpret news events, historical images, and text to create a visual diary focusing on a specific story or occurrence. My images are used to preserve the collective memory of this society and focus on events that appear to be ordinary and horrific. Creating visual diaries through photo quilts is a means of telling stories, which follows the tradition of African American story quilts. Quilts are made to remind us who we are, and who and what our ancestors have been to us and the larger society.

Marie Wilson
Brooklyn, New York

WITH MY "contemporary tapestries," I try to illustrate connections between people and events. Everywhere in the world, we do the same things, using what is available to us. We feed and clothe our families, travel from one place to another, and create art. Using colors, shapes, and textures, I like to stitch together stories about our universal efforts. I use lace for clouds, ribbons for rivers, velvet for rocks, and I embroider music throughout these images. It's a very satisfactory way to spend time. If I'm displeased with the world I'm looking at, I create another one.

When a viewer looks at my work, I don't want that person to be aware of the research, the glitches, the geometry, or the midnight prayers and curses that have gone into the work. I simply hope that it will be appealing to look at.

ABOVE: *Detail from "Summer's Splendor"*

Index